THE

TUPAC

CODE

Written by: Marc Shyst

TABLE OF CONTENTS

CHAPTER 1

PROPHECY OF HIP HOP

(Revelation 1:3)

Blessed is he that readeth, and they that hear the words of this prophecy, and keep those things which are written therein: for the time is at hand

When you think of hip hop the first thing that comes to mind to many is loud music, expensive clothes and wild teenagers. This is the modern stereotype of what hip hop has become. In most of today's society, the outside view of hip hop is only a fad of the evolving culture. When you look at TV today, you can see how corporate America has targeted certain markets as they use hip hop beats and rhymes in their commercials to gain the attention of the hip hop community. Radio stations bring in millions of dollars every year off of advertisement ads to the hip hop community. Corporate America has statistically found a way to advertise to the billions of consumer's everyday not just through TV but through radio also. So when you decide to listen to your favorite radio station, remember this, you have now locked yourself in with a program of statistics and strategies to persuade your consumer purchases of music, cars, clothes, and food. The bottom line of this explanation is that now more than ever in America hip hop is a big business.

If you look into the history of hip hop you'll find that its substance is much stronger and deeper than just business. In the beginning of time before there was a heaven or earth there was the word. The word was God, and he spoke the word and said let there be light and there was light. He saw that the light was good and it divided the dark. He called the light day and he called the dark night. In truth that's how this world was created from the spoken word. From there he created the heavens and earth and then came communication, which brought us praise and worship through song. Throughout the Bible there are numerous occasions where God has ordered his prophets to assemble choirs to sing before battle, to usher in the spirit of the Lord and overcome adversity to victory. To no consequence, it would be the same spoken word that thousands of years later would be the underground way of communication for slaves during slavery. Many today may look at what we as African Americans have been through with slavery as the worst thing in the world that could happen to a nation of people. From my insight and what the Lord has shared with me, I feel blessed and honored to be a product of what my ancestors fought and died for. The children of Israel were Gods chosen people that he led out of slavery into the promise land that he made provisions for. I've always felt that the Africans that where brought out of the country and brought to America as slaves were also Gods chosen people. I know for sure he has given us the same promised glory as the children of Israel. Just like Israel it's up to us to believe in him and his son Jesus to completely come into the promised inheritance. I look at what my ancestors went through, and it's the cornerstone that would bring us to where we are today. Slaves would sing hymns with coded messages amongst the other slaves. These hymns would also be comfort and inspiration to the slaves in troubled times. Slaves were known to gather in ciphers to share stories and fellowship in song to keep each other motivated. It is also my belief that the inheritance of the kings and queens from Africa has evolved into what you now see today as hip hop. From what we were stripped of, hip hop is what we have *built, made, and created to be a blessing.*

Today hip hop has become less of an art but more of a full contact sport. The competiveness to be number one or better than your opponent has now become the main event of hip hop. This competitive spirit can be traced back to the world famous artists Leonardo and Michelangelo, when words of poetic speeches of disrespect were said before revealing their paintings because it was said that their paintings sometimes were similar. There was said to be altercations and riots at the painting premiers, due to differences in opinion of who was the best artist. Later as Jazz music would evolve in America, two jazz greats would be the center of competition of their era. Their names were Bird and Coltrane. Competiveness is a motivational tool used to bring the best out of competing opponents, but could this competiveness also bring out the wickedness of a competitor in order to win?

With the progression of the United States of America, there was a silent reality in the community of African Americans that lived in poverty. Along with freedom of slavery came the mistreatment of African

Americans. A lot of African Americans were subjected to poor living environments, low income jobs, treated as outcasts and even being lynched and burned in public. Out of this injustice came the voices of some of our nation's strongest leaders such as Martin Luther King Jr. and Malcom X. Where there is injustice and a need for awareness, God always raises a prophet of his generation to lead a movement of righteousness. Later would arise the movement of the Black Panther Party, a revolutionary party that not only spoke for the injustice in the black community but stood against it. The struggles and poverty of African Americans has stood the test of time.

This culture of poverty would eventually surface to America as hip hop. The voices of hip hop would derive from the view of the affected people of those communities. If ever a revolution was to be started, I believe it began when hip hop was born. Hip hop was born in the inner city to give the underprivileged a way to be heard and express feelings of love, peace and truth of reality. Through time and effort hip hop's competiveness has brought about righteousness in the fact that it has always been the voice of the neglected, but it also has brought out wickedness because people would say anything through spoken word in order to be number one. The first monumental battle of hip hop that was the turning point of its era came in 1981, when Kool Moe Dee dissed Busy Bee at a competition in Harlem, NY. That one turning point gave way to the hip hop art form of battling. The art of battling is most righteously utilized when another artist exposes truth from lies over rhyme and beat. One of the all-time righteous battles of hip hop came in the 80's when KRS ONE of Boogie Down Productions dissed MC Shan, who made a song called Queens Bridge, which stated that's where hip hop started in Queens Bridge. The battle sparked truth in the culture when KRS ONE released a song called South Bronx, claiming that hip hop originated in Bronx, NY. MC Shan and KRS ONE are till this day major legends in hip hop because of this battle. In the process of the battle it gave witness to a revolution. A revolution to deliver truth by KRS ONE that hip hop started in Bronx NY with Kool Hurk. Both MC Shan and KRS ONE are still friends to this day and have a mutual respect for each other.

Over time many MC's have battled but not to the extent of righteousness in hip hop, but in differences of

opinions that has brought forth wickedness. In the era of
hip hop battling, it has sparked a trend where there would
be ciphers of rappers gathered together showing their skill
by dissing an opponent. As hip hop spread across the
country from NY to LA, the evolution of hip hop began to
change. The west coast would bring the era of gangster
rap to hip hop with a group out of Compton, California
called NWA (Niggas with Attitudes). The events that took
place after the success of this west coast label would
change the direction of hip hop. After having platinum
success in album sales, one of the members of NWA by the
name of ICE CUBE refused to sign the labels contract and
advancements. ICE CUBE'S insubordination was derived
from the inadequate amount of money divided by the
group. ICE CUBE left the group feeling as if he wasn't
getting his righteous share for the work he had done. This
split from the group would become one of the first battles
to pursue between former business partners and friends.
NWA released songs dissing ICE CUBE for leaving the group
and ICE CUBE released songs dissing NWA for doing him
injustice. While the New York hip hop scene was on the
rise, the altercations of NWA and the rise of west coast hip

hop would all affect each other in a future chain of events. While NWA was feuding on the west coast, a lot of independent labels out of New York were emerging into hip hop and having success. One of these labels would be Bad Boy Records. After the departure of ICE CUBE from NWA, the producer from NWA by the name of DR. DRE would also leave the label due to not receiving his fair pay from work that was done. DR. DRE's departure lead him to start his own record label with a body guard by the name of Suge Knight. What would follow after this departure by DR. DRE would be a fuel of diss songs by CEO of NWA, EASY E. DR. DRE retaliated by forming the label Death Row Records with Suge Knight, followed by an onslaught of diss songs against EASY E.

While the rise of hip hop was now at an all-time high in the early 90's on the west coast, there was an east coast rapper by the name of Tupac Shakur who was on his way to be a legend in the prophecy of hip hop. Tupac Shakur was born in Brooklyn, NY, but moved and was raised in Baltimore, Maryland. During the 90's Tupac moved from Baltimore, MD to California with his mother to escape the harsh treatment and surveillance by the FBI because she was a member of the Black Panther Party. As his career as a rapper blossomed so did his affiliation with his east coast acquaintances and west coast acquaintances. While pursuing his career as a rapper, Tupac became acquaintances with an east coast rapper by the name of Biggie Smalls. Biggie Smalls was the newest rapper on the east coast label Bad Boy Records, which was run by Sean Puff Daddy Combs. The friendship between Tupac and Biggie would all come to an exploding tragedy when Tupac was robbed and shot in the lobby of New York's Quad Studios where his affiliates Biggie Smalls and Puff Daddy were also in attendance. After this robbery and shooting, hip hop as the world knew it would forever be changed. Tupac survived the robbery and shooting and claimed that Puffy and Biggie of Bad Boy Records set him up to be killed. While recovering from his gunshot wounds the young rapper, Tupac Shakur was facing non related charges for rape. The feud of Tupac and Bad Boy was now in the media of hip hop's spot light. After the shooting Tupac was found guilty of the rape charges and sentenced to jail. While in jail the accusations of him being set up by Biggie and Puffy floated heavily through hip hop and in *personal interviews.*

After serving nine months in jail, the rapper Tupac Shakur signed a major record deal directly from jail with Suge Knight, CEO of the newly started west coast record label, Death Row Records. Suge Knight agreed to pay Tupac's bail bond of one million dollars. In return he signed with Death Row Records. What followed after the release of Tupac from jail would be a media explosion. Tupac having felt that he was set up and double crossed by his affiliates Biggie Smalls and Puff Daddy, quickly began to attack the character of Biggie and Puffy in the media and on record. These disses would ignite one of the biggest beefs and battles in hip hop today. Tupac being on a west coast record label and Biggie Smalls being on an east coast label, made a media frenzy and turned the attention to an east coast and west coast beef and battle. This battle was followed by an all-time diss by Tupac on Biggie called Hit Em Up, were he taunted his character and insulted his wife and record label. Biggie Smalls in this heated battle never responded directly to any of Tupac's' disses, but was thought to have sent a subliminal message in a song called, Who Shot Ya. With both rappers record labels under the media eye of hip hop, there were a few incidents

of confrontations between the two labels and rappers

where fatal gunshot wounds were reported.

In September of 1996, Tupac Shakur was fatally

injured in a gun shooting after leaving a Mike Tyson fight

in Las Vegas. Nevada. Tupac died from his injuries six days

later in the University Medical Center of Southern, Nevada.

After the death of Tupac there was speculation that Bad

Boy Records may have orchestrated the shooting, but was

later declared false by investigating police. Nine months

after the death of Tupac in Las Vegas, Nevada, Biggie

Smalls was fatally shot coming from an album release

party in Los Angeles, California. He was pronounced dead

on arrival when he was brought in to Cedars-Sinai Medical

Center. Investigators of the Biggie Small shooting found

evidence in the murder case that point to Death Row

Records, but after key evidence was dropped from the

case, the Los Angeles police department declared the

murder unsolved. As with the murder case of Tupac

Shakur no one was ever charged in the murder of Biggie

Smalls and the Los Angeles police department declared the

murder unsolved. With the untimely deaths of Tupac and

Biggie, these incidents give witness to the seriousness of beef and battling in hip hop. Has hip hop learned from this tragedy or is the wickedness in hip hop stronger because of beef and battles?

CHAPTER 2

BIRTH OF A PROPHET

(Deuteronomy 18:18)

I will raise them up a Prophet from among their brethren, like unto thee, and will put my words in his mouth; and he shall speak unto them all that I shall command him

When the prophet, Christ Jesus was born to the world, his birth was one of a miracle. The prophet Jesus was Gods Son, his self in human form. His mother Mary, was a chosen virgin, who gave birth to this Immaculate Conception. His mission on this earth was to suffer the sin, and save the souls of man. The prophecy of Christ Jesus was the reason and purpose for the messages of those prophets before him. Those before him prophesized he was coming, and now as he has come, suffered and died as a sacrifice for though we may live. It is the purpose of the prophets after him to use our lives to testify he lived, died, and has risen and is coming back again. In my faith in the Lord Jesus, I believe if we trust in him and follow his way to glory, we will suffer his sufferings in order to stand in his victory.

Before it's said who is a prophet, we may recognize it by the miracle of his birth as a witness. So now I'll take you to a confused young African American mother with one daughter who's struggling to take care of her child and family. The mother whose name is Mary became pregnant with her second child and had doubts of being able to financially support the addition to her family. The thought of an abortion was in action until a conversation with what I felt was a messenger, with my Aunt Odessa, gave her the faith to proceed to give birth and let God provide. So on April 27th, at Columbia Hospital for Women in Washington, D.C., Mary went into labor with her baby. The delivery went tragic when the umbilical cord was wrapped around the neck of her baby. Doctors feared the baby would suffocate and die, but the cord was miraculously untangled and she gave birth to her only son. That son she gave birth to was me. And that's the truth of the root of my birth. The seed was planted to suffer the flesh for reasons unknown to him at the time. To take you to the pain we'll start at eleven years old and I'm just meeting my fathers' father. We were introduced by my grandmother at my father's funeral. My grandfather wasn't around much in my father's life, and had little involvement in it. As the same way my father wasn't there for me, so this was an awkward moment for me to meet my grandfather for the first time here at my father's funeral. I remember a smooth clean cut sugar daddy looking dude. He lived in Baltimore and no one ever saw much of him. He had on sun shades so I never saw his eyes as he rode with us in the limousine with the family going to my father's funeral. As we were in route to the funeral, I was thinking to myself, is this how I'm going to look when I'm an old man and with grandchildren, or am I going to be different and know my child. At the funeral I just sat there with the frown of a frustrated kid. I wanted to cry like I missed my father, but I couldn't miss what was hardly there. That was the first and last time I'd ever see my grandfather alive, he passed away some years later in Baltimore.

As the years went by, a lot of things in life were happening in the world of hip hop. I used to be a big fan of RUN DMC and Jam Master Jay, LL Cool J, Salt 'N Pepper and all of the rappers of that era. Can you imagine growing up feeling like a loner to the world without a father and the only thing that gave you comfort was music, art and basketball. By the time I was in elementary school, I had adapted myself to take care of myself and protect myself from hurt. When you move around a lot as a kid you're always the new kid on the block, and that meant either adapting with others to fit in with these new people or stay to myself and not get affiliated. More than the first option I chose to stay to myself and let my friends come to me. Being a fatherless child and seeing how my mother struggled so much to make ends meet, I never really trusted anyone or anything of that matter that could let me down any more than I had already been let down in life. All my life as a kid I dreamed of playing professional basketball in the NBA, that hoop dream gave me faith that one day I could make things better for my mom. My harsh reality in the situation was that I was always a good basketball player but suffered from a lack of male guidance and discipline for myself to become a professional. In the early 90's when rappers like Snoop Dogg and the Ghetto Boys were out, I was being cut from my JR High basketball team and thinking, how else am I going to make it in this world outside of basketball?

During my junior high school years I listened to a lot of music in my room and anywhere else I could play a tape. You know how when you start talking to girls on the phone and thinking you're grown, that was me. I use to listen to the slow songs by groups like Jodeci and H Town, thinking about what I'm going do when I do get me a girlfriend and how I'm going to do it. Music was the everyday thing that calmed the suffering of poverty. While in JR High the movie Juice came out, I remember like yesterday how my childhood friends and I caught the train to go see the movie. We scrounged up enough money for one another and bought our tickets into the theater. After we saw that movie we swore up and down that was us and how we lived. Truthfully it was how we really lived every day in our hood. Everybody wanted to be like Bishop in the movie, a character played by Tupac Shakur. For me myself this was the first time seeing or even hearing of this dude Tupac when I saw the movie. Later I found out he was a rapper and checked out his music. When I heard Tupac it was like hearing words from the brother that I was separated from at birth. I mean it was just so fascinating how someone I never met could have so much in common about our life.

Tupac spoke to my soul through his music and gave me all the motivation I needed to not give up on life. It was then that music was a fellowship and not just a song to me anymore.

As I matured through my childhood years I found myself still following my hoop dreams and with every Tupac compact disc that was out. By the time I was in high school, the innocents of my childhood and the pressures of the inner city environment had caught up with me. I had just went out for the JR varsity tryouts and didn't make the cut. After not making the cut that year, I played recreation basketball and stayed focused on the dream. Playing recreation is good but not like playing school ball, where you're being taught discipline and knowledge. When you're playing rec ball, it's like the referee not on the court, dudes fouling, traveling, and everybody trying play like Jordan. When I played rec ball, I use to listen to my Walkman before every game, that's how I got pumped. That's when Scarface dropped his cd called THE DIARY, that's what I played before every game. While still playing rec ball meant playing street ball and playing street ball kept me in the street. Everybody that was at the rec were considered the hustlers from the neighborhood, and that's where they met up, kicked it and shot ball. After a while the season was over, and we were still meeting up. That's when the extracurricular activities of the streets came in, and basketball was no longer a dream but a reality that I might not make it. Although the reality in this case could have been conquered and achieved had I'd been lead through it with the right leadership, but I wasn't. I still played ball and tried out at school, but I was surrounded by peers who all had the same dream to make it out the hood by playing ball, and being like Jordan. We all knew that all of us weren't going to make it, so the street life kept us occupied and uplifted about being something in life and not failing. I was at that point in high school though, I was hustling after school to take care of myself, you know just enough to eat and keep my shoes fresh. I wasn't on a king pin, lock down the block type shit, that's just what it was to survive, and I adapted. When the streets came into my life I was still at home with my mom, by that time I was listening to the west coast real hard, Snoop Dog, Tha Dog Pound and Mc eight. When at home I would close my door and play my music loud like I was in an apartment of my *own, and at home it's live in moms' house, live by moms'*

rules. That was cool and all that, nothing special that

every child can't handle in loving your parents, for me

though I had to leave. I left home after my tenth grade

year of high school for more reasons than expressed, not

because I was kicked out or anything, it was just too much

suffering on my mother for me to continue to be a load on.

I just wanted to release myself from bondage and live the

life destined for me. So I left home at sixteen and moved

out of town with a relative in Virginia. Where I moved to

was the total opposite of my surroundings in the city, it

was the country. The new surroundings brought new

opportunities, at least that's what I sold my mom on in

order to convince her to let me move out. When I moved

out, I had to register for school and get enrolled back in.

Being in a new school brought back my opportunity to

make it with basketball again. So for a minute I was

focused and on track, I tried out for the basketball team

and made tryouts. After I made the team I felt that the

dream once again was a reality that I might possibly have

a chance to make it. While I had all the opportunity in the

world to progress with basketball, I still didn't have the influential guidance once again that was needed to progress. I was really living on my own and going to school. I would live at different family members' houses for a while then move with another, that's how it was for me for a while. It was all love from my family to be there, but imagine me having to first find a way to school every day, and then going to after school practice, and then leaving to who knows house that night to do the hardest homework you could give a high school student. On top of all that, the street life that I had adapted to in the city was now my means of survival on my own. Within all the confusion of it all, I was the most talented player on the team. All the other players were from the country and were used to a more fundamental style of playing basketball. I was like Jordan for real at my new school, the coach loved me, he used to tell me in the games sometimes "Give them that D.C. crossover" and I would do something fancy on the court and shake the player up. At the new school, things couldn't get any better, but at the same time it seemed like things couldn't get any worse. In all truth about the situation I have never in my life felt the things that I had felt going to a suburban school in Virginia. In

D.C. it was heavily populated with all African American students, it was the ghetto and everyone knew nothing else. With the new change of school came the new change of environment. At my new school there were more white kids than African American, there were only like twenty percent African American, the other eighty percent was all white. It was cool to see the differences, but it wasn't cool to feel the differences. See in the area in Virginia I was in, there still lived prejudice, this wasn't an out front thing that was seen, it was just an uneasy feeling that was felt in the community. You can usually tell the way parents are by the way their kids act, and at my new school there where a lot of prejudice kids who knew no better than to look down on African Americans. It was like, in school there was separation of the races, the white kids did one thing and the African Americans did another. Even at lunch, you would rarely see African Americans and whites together, it would always be one table in the lunch room with nothing but African Americans and white kids stayed at their tables. So as you can imagine, me being an African American student with more talent in my pinky finger than any of the white basketball players, that there would be problems. The principal was a white man named Mr. Jury, if you asked the white kids at that school about him, they would say he was an asshole, and if you asked any African American kid, they would say that he was prejudice. I, myself think he was both, I used to watch how he interacted with the students to find prejudice, and what I found is that most prejudice people can act and deal with people outside their race for a while but their true ways come out. Mr. Jury just seemed to give the African American students a harder time than he did others, everyone knew this but couldn't ever find fault and evidence enough to loudly protest. Mr. Jury kept his close eye on me the whole time I was enrolled. He had this inner city stereotype about me that I was trouble, he was right but I never gave that school a chance to see it. I acted as an angel in school with proper manners and respect always, it kept Mr. Jury curious to who I was.

In my twelfth and final year to graduate, I knew this was my opportunity to ever make it to the next level in my basketball career. By now I had survived a year away from home and actually passed, but the back and forth of living with different people and still living the street life of a hustler finally hit the fan with Mr. Jury's' prejudice. During the beginning of the new basketball season, I was called out of basketball practice to the principal's office. On the way to the office I thought to myself what in the world could it be that they needed me this bad for? When I got in the office it was none other than Mr. Jury, and with the evilest smile on his face he notified me that he had received a call from my probation officer at the time and was notified of an out of area address. The whole matter was nothing serious, I explained to him that the address that she had was a temporary one of a relative that I was staying with at the time. That's when the evilness in his intentions were exposed, so with an evil smile of sarcasm he notified me that I was going to have to leave that school and register in the county of the address of my relative. I debated with him back and forth about it and left out of his office mad and went and finished practice. After the incident, Mr. Jury made it very clear to me that if I got to school late, I would have to sit out of the game that many minutes I was late in order to play. This was an unfair and unjust way of disciplining a basketball player. The first time I was late ten minutes to school, he had the *coach sit me on the bench the first ten minutes of the game without playing. This kind of tactic he was playing with me was obviously his way of just keeping me from participating in the season and not receiving my scholarship. I stayed focus on school and basketball as I was supposed to, and before every game I still listened to my Walkman to get me pumped up. My music was the only thing that kept me comforted when I was away. That's when Tupac dropped ALL EYES ON ME, I remember being in Virginia when he was shot and killed, it was a life changing tragedy in my life. I just knew it could happen to anyone when it happened to Pac. So it was a few games into the season and this was my second time being late to school since the discussion. When I got to school Mr. Jury laughingly made the comment, "You know what this means, no playing time for you", and at that moment in my life I could no longer go on playing this game with this prejudice environment of people, so I told the Mr. Jury "Man don't even worry about the game, just give me my transfer papers, you won the battle but not the war." That day was one of the most defying moments in my life, because I felt like I had everything there to make it and I was about to lose everything now. On the other hand I felt like I just made the best move of my life and as such must move on from the situation, and I did just that. I got my transfer papers and left my dream behind in Virginia and moved back home to the city.*

When I moved back to the city, I had left the dream behind and it was University of Hard Knocks that I attended now. I left that school in the country of Virginia and for the sake of getting my diploma I registered at a close by school in northern Virginia, in Arlington County, more of a city like atmosphere. I finished my senior year at the new school and had to receive my finishing credits at summer school. With that being said, I shouldn't have to tell you how hard it was for me not to be able to graduate with my classmates and walk across the stage. It was like torture that summer for me to be in school all day when I felt I was supposed to be having the time of my life as a free student. After finishing a long summer of school it was finally over and I felt that I had accomplished the long hurdle that was in front of me. When the new school in Virginia got in contact with the previous school I attended in the country of Virginia to gather my credit score for my diploma, they were notified that I had not earned enough credits from the old school in Virginia that were earlier estimated. This to me was another attempt of Mr. Jury to just make sure injustice was served on me. When I got the news from my school that I was just one credit short to receive my diploma I was furious and in rage about it, I was in so much confusion and disbelief that I made my mind up that after how hard I tried to do right and graduate and for this to happen, that I wasn't going back another year for just one credit. I made a bold decision and refused to go back to school for another year. For a while I felt like I had let the game beat me, like I didn't make the right decisions and things didn't go my way. After a few thoughts of feeling down, my motivation would be rekindled by thoughts of the street life. See in all the years of my life sacrificing not being involved with the street life for my dreams, the moment I got in, it was evident that it was there waiting for me. One of the things that lure you in the life of the streets is that you get some of the materialistic things of that of someone who is successful. When I got a little money saved up I got myself most of the things I didn't have when I was younger, so you could *imagine all the clothes and shoes I had. I had some of the material things of success but I didn't have a legitimate plan for success much less an organized plan. The street life brought me a lot of ups and downs, but that's just what comes with that lifestyle. When I was running the streets hustling, music was my theme for everything. I was still listening to my Tupac CD's and a lot of other rappers who were out at that time. During those years I use to like the new era of hip hop that was on the rise like Ja Rule and Memphis Bleek, all the music that I listened to was influential to my life style. I wasn't doing nothing anyone said in a song but everything they talked about in their songs I was living, that kept my music apart of my fellowship.*

While I was out of school and hustling, I remember one day in a dazed out thought thinking about my diploma. It had now been a whole year since I had left high school. The thought of this outrageous situation made me investigate just to give rest to my theory of injustice. So I had my mother call the country school in Virginia to verify my credits and when she did the information came back that I did have enough credits to receive a diploma. After a year wait I was awarded my high school diploma from Washington Lee high school in Arlington Virginia. That was good and all but I still had a one track mind of the streets. Now I really was on my own, and this is the path that I had now chosen to find success.

CHAPTER 3

CHANGE OF EVENTS 9-11-01

(James 1:12)

Blessed is the man that endureth temptation for when he is tried, he shall receive the crown of life, which the Lord hath promise to them that love him.

It's September 9, 2001 and I'm being awakened out of my sleep at 4:00 a.m. by the jail C.O.., telling me I'm due in court today. I woke up with a mean look of confusion on my face to the C.O. like, what'? Go to court? My lawyer never said anything about me having court today. The C.O. looked over his list again and said "Yup it says it right here, you go to court today for appeal." Now this would have been good news if I had only been locked up for two weeks, but I was due to be released to go home in two weeks. My first thoughts about going to appeal were negative and disbelief, but after being locked up for six months, you'll go about anywhere to get out of the cell and to see the world, so I went. When you go to court in jail it's an all-day herd of back and forth checking and transport. While getting processed from the jail that morning I remember thinking that my lawyers are the most unbelievable disappointing people in this world to have me arraigned for appeal today and I go home in two weeks. They were about six months late. By this time in my life, the lawyer I had retained knew me very well. I had retained him two times before on non-related cases, so he knew my path of trouble. As we were on the transportation van going to court it was a feeling like no other. After being locked up for the last six months, this was my first time getting outside of the jail walls. With only two weeks left, I thought that it would be nice to get out two weeks earlier and go home.

Just thinking about going home gave me the chance to reflect on what I had been through while in jail. I know this may seem crazy, but jail for me was the best thing that could have happened to me at that time in my life. I know it was Gods way of setting me down and getting my life focused. At the jail where I served my time in Virginia, there were a lot of federal inmates amongst local state inmates. This was against all federal and state law constitution of inmates. Truthfully, the jail was receiving government money for holding federal inmates and housing them with the state inmates, due to overcrowding. Now this for most would have been a problem, but not for me at that time. When I first got to jail my motive was to find me a major drug connect and get out and go harder on the streets than I did before. That was my plan, but another thing happened to me. After getting familiar with the jail policies and procedures, I requested a job to occupy my time. I signed up to be a barber because that's what I knew how to do in the streets, so I figured I could do it in jail. A few days after filling out the request, the job slip came back that I got the job and would be moving out of my section to the trustee section. The next day a correctional officer came that evening with a transfer cart and called for me and a few other inmates in that section to get our things to be moved to the trustee section.

I was real distant with everybody and kept to myself in jail, but in this new trustee section it was more relaxed and civilized. The atmosphere was totally different because of the different treatment. The trustee section was where they housed all the inmates who had jobs in jail and all the inmates who were on work release. This meant that they had a little more leniency than the other inmates.

One particular thing different in the trustee section was the food you ate. In the rest of the jail the servings of the food were small, so small that after you finished eating, you were full but man another tray would do you justice. Not in the trustee section, they received a double serving of everything, not because the jail gave it to them, it was that the inmates in the kitchen prepared all the trays, so when they fixed our section, they just looked out. When I was transferred to the trustee section they had just served dinner so I didn't eat in there the first day. The next morning when breakfast trays came through I was awakened out of my sleep by someone hollering "Trays" and when I got up to get my tray, you would have thought it was a tray prepared by IHOP, I had double of everything, I ate so much that first morning that I stuffed myself too much and threw up. That was my first lesson in jail about a soldier's conduct. After being in the new section for a few days I started to get the hang of the jail procedures. Even though I was learning to respect the situation that I was in, I still was holding on to a lot of aggression and anger. This aggression and anger would soon land me in positions of corrections. It was like my fifth day in my new section of the jail, and the jail had not yet replaced my name and identification for me to receive my trays when they came. So every time the trays would come, instead of my name being called like everyone else, I just waited until they called barber. On this particular day though I was in my jail house mood, and they didn't call my tray, so I asked the correctional officer about my tray as they were being distributed and he in return told me to wait until all the trays were called, and I did. At this point though, in my own little mind I felt disrespected that I had to wait, so by the time trays were distributed I was the last one to get mine. So to show my frustration, while the correctional officer was standing in front of me, I took the uneaten tray and threw it up on the shelf, when the correctional officer looked up at me, I just gave him a serious look in my eyes and gritted on him then walked off. It would have been one thing to just disrespect a correctional officer but the officer I gritted on was the captain of the jail, this was another one of my newcomer lessons that I was taught. After I gritted on him and started walking off, out of nowhere he started ramping and raving, screaming at the top of his lungs, "I know what that look means, I'm from the same streets you're from, you getting out of here." Me being the con artist I was, I stopped and looked at him and was like "What you talking about, I didn't even say nothing." Everyone in the section was like Marc what happened, what you do, and I just played it off like he was tripping. Sure enough, about five minutes later two guards came with another transfer cart and escorted me out. Now at that time I was the only barber in the jail so there wasn't anybody else to cut the inmates hair. After they escorted me out, I was taken to booking and placed me in a holding cell. The whole time I was in the holding cell I was angry and furious. I paced back and forth in the cell the whole time thinking to myself where are these jerks going to move me to now? I really wasn't worried in fear, I just had other enemies in that jail and if I was to get put in the same section as them it would have been on. So the whole time in the holding cell I was doing pushups and getting myself pumped up to fight if I had to. Waiting in that cell was like someone waiting on death row to be executed. They took forever and then they finally sent an officer to take me to my new location. When they came and got me I was breathing hard and looking like I just was training for *a championship fight. The captain did something to me that he thought was going to break me. He had me sent to the smallest section in the jail called G pod. G pod is where all the grown and aggressive inmates were. There was no playing in this section, it was all mean mugs and muscle. The G pod was so small it only held like 16 inmates, compared to the trustee section that held 80 inmates. When I got in there, I just kept a tight face and went to my bunk and got situated. As I was placing all my stuff in my locker everyone could see my canteen bag with all my snacks, then I heard a voice say in a joking manner "We gone eat good tonight." I turned around as fast as I could to see who had said anything and it was a group of older men talking with each other but they saw me look at them and just kept talking as if to say they didn't say anything. I just unloaded my things and said to myself if anyone tries to steal my canteen tonight. Whoever it is I hope they willing to die for it, because that's what it's going to be if I catch them trying to steal my canteen. After I got settled that day I kept my eye on everyone in there, then I thought to myself, these old heads probably think that's real funny, I kind of figured they were just trying to see if I was scared.*

That night it was all good, no one tried to steal my canteen. G pod was a good thing for me. The captain thought that I would be intimidated by the more aggressive part of the jail but it was just the opposite, I adapted to the aggressiveness and found home in there. After a week in that section it was like my new home, I had connected with just about all the inmates in the section and they respected me for being me. One of my inmates in G pod was a Jamaican named Black. I would always ask Black about getting me some weed when I got out and helping me get on, but Black would never give in to me, he would always say "Read your bible mon, don't think about that life, read your bible and think good thoughts mon". Black was funny to me because he was in jail for guns and a whole lot of other drug charges, he was doing twelve years and his new outlook on life was different. I remember one day I asked Black again for the weed connect and he got frustrated with me and was like "How much you want mon"? When he asked me I was kind of in shock and answered like "About ten pounds." When I said that, Black was heated and said "Mon, I only deal with one hundred pounds or better, can you handle that?" I just stared laughing at him because he was trying to be serious and I just found humor in him because he had changed the way he thought about hustling. After I was laughing at him, Black told me with a smile on his face "Mon all the money I was making when I was home means nothing to me in here. If I could get out of here and be free, I would be happy with working all day for one dollar mon!! One dollar!" The thing about Black I respected is that he never gave any bad advice, he always gave me a good word of encouragement and wisdom. On Sundays in jail I started going to church services to stay positive.

While the captain of the jail was trying to teach me a lesson, the jail was suffering because there was no one to cut the inmates hair. I guess he figured someone would sign up for the job, but they didn't and the job went vacant. All the inmates in the whole jail would walk pass and see me in the new section and be like "when you going back to the trustee section so you can cut hair, we hurting." I never really planned on going back to cutting hair in there again, but after two weeks of no one in the entire jail having haircuts, the captain sent for me and had me brought back to the trustee section and continue to cut hair. When I got back to the trustee section I was like a new man. Everyone in the trustee section was walking around talking and more social than G pod. One of my peoples from the street was like you all right Marc, and I didn't even open my mouth, I just nodded my head yes and kept unpacking my things. I was still the same person, I just had another view on this whole situation of jail now and it was serious to me. The time in G pod made me more focused.

When I came back to the trustee section, I just knew I had to take advantage of the opportunity and freedom I had in there. The special thing about the trustee section was that they held their own church service every day at seven o'clock. The service was more of a bible study fellowship by a federal inmate who took it upon himself as a messenger of God to minister to souls in jail. In all truth, I never went to the fellowship meetings, I would always just watch them or be doing something else when they had fellowship. A few days after being back in the trustee section I was asleep in my bed when, in my dreams, I could hear someone speaking words of truth from God about getting your life together to get out and be a productive member of society and not waste your life in jail. The message that the inmate was preaching hit me in my sleep and I woke up and just sat on my bunk with a tear in my eye and a knot in my heart. I said to myself, got to go and fellowship with these brothers and get my soul right. The next day I went to the fellowship meeting at seven o'clock and it was my destiny to be there. The jail ministers name was Pervall, he was from Richmond, V.A. and had been locked up, got out and went back to the same life and got locked up again. Pervall was real short and small, he stood about 5'2 and had a muscular build with a bald head. You could tell he was a gangster but he had changed his life for God and was thorough with his messages. Pervall felt it was his calling, while in jail, to minister the word of God. After meeting Pervall and talking with him, he was like the older brother I never had and he took special interest in me. While talking to Pervall he told me he had a conversation with the captain of the jail and spoke with him about getting me back over into the trustee section. Pervall told me that the captain said he knew I was a good dude but that when I looked at him and gritted on him, he said I had a look in my eyes as if I could have killed him and *he wanted to teach me a lesson. While talking with Pervall I started to understand more about the conduct of a man and what it could lead to, not only in jail, but on the streets. When I took the responsibility of God's word, I fellowshipped everyday with my section in jail and fed my spirit.*

Once I got back into the regular routine of cutting hair again, I really saw and felt how much my presence meant to the whole jail. See, out of all the jobs in the jail, the barber had it the best but the worst. I say that in understanding that no other job was called to be interactive with the inmates in jail. I was in touch with everybody and everybody was in touch with me. So I started taking on the job as my own personal way of doing God's work by being the soul who cut the criminals hair and touch them in my own way to give a sense of hope with just a haircut. While cutting hair one day, the captain who kicked me out was walking through the hallway where I was. I apologized and we made peace with each other. The peace that was made was more so for my soul and not to hold any anger and grudges towards another man. After that, I felt I was learning greater things than

any man could ever know. It was about life and how to
survive. While continuing in bible study, I told Pervall one
day, that I wanted to start reading the bible and where
should I start. I remember Pervall telling me kindly to start
reading at the New Testament cause that's where I would
understand. So that night on my bunk before I opened up
my bible and read, I asked God to lead me, and he directed
me to open up and start reading at the beginning of the
bible. That night my spirit was ignited and I was inspired
by the things I read. What followed the rest of my time in
jail was an everyday fellowship that gave me the wisdom
to be stronger in life.

CHAPTER 4

ORCHESTR8ED PRODUCTION

(ECCLESIASTES 3:1)

There is a time for everything and a season for every activity under the heavens.

While incarcerated in Virginia, all I wanted was to get out and back to writing to beats and get in the studio with my producer, Rodney and his man, Shamar. I talked with Rodney on the phone from jail a few times and I remember Shamar in the background yelling out "man we gone come break you out there Shyst" in a joking manner. At the time it encouraged me and I stayed focused on my plan for once I got out of jail. Once I knew my release date, I was counting down. I had a release date for September 25th and I couldn't wait. On September 7th, mail call came in as usual and I can never forget it. Ms. Thorn, who we called Rick Flair because she was a white woman who had manly features with gold blond curls in her hair yelled, "Ball, Mail!" I walked over to the booth she was in only to read a note from the jail saying my new release date was

September 28th. I was so disappointed that it made me damn near sick. I couldn't believe it. I went and laid in my bunk all morning until dinner came. All day I stayed silent with a tight face and didn't talk to anybody. The only positive I could see in this is that I was scheduled to get baptized in jail on the 26th and now that I wasn't going home, I could be baptized. God knows my heart, and as much as I wanted to go home it was still hard to swallow still being in jail 3 more days than I thought I would be. That particular day when I got the news I wasn't getting released until the 28th, I was chosen by Pervall to lead the bible study. I testified to the bible study of my distress and how the positive was that now I would be getting baptized in jail. The news uplifted all the inmates in bible study and it brought a sense of comfort to me to accept it for the good. I lead the bible study with a word and we closed out as normal. In the days following on the 26th the C.O.. called for church, and as we stood with bibles in our hand to meet in the law library. I felt like I was waiting to go into a main event championship basketball game and I was the star player on my squad. The service was awesome, Reverend Murphy baptized me in the name of the Father and of the Son, and of the Holy Spirit. As he poured water on my head I was made a new man. All things of old were washed away. On September 28th I awoke to breakfast trays, and after breakfast I stayed up to be released. As I waited my stomach began to jump and rumble in nervous anticipation thinking was this really going down today? As I sat there, at about 10am the C.O. called for me and I said my peace to all the inmates I knew and was released a free man.

Once home, the first day all I had on my mind was getting to my music and making things happen out in the world. I was focused on my music and making a way for myself and my family. After 2 days I made myself over to Rodney's house in Suitland, Maryland. Rodney was still at the same place in Hill Top Apartments. I was excited as I was heading over his house, I called him up and let him know I was on my way over. When I got there, Rodney answered and let me in. I yelled out "Hott Rod" and he yelled out "Shyst", we both embraced like two brothers meeting for the first time. As I came in I saw his man George sitting on the couch, playing the game, I greeted George with a hand shake, but once I saw him there, in the

back of my mind I was like "Aww shit." Before I went in
George would come over with Rodney and play Madden
and smoke, which was their bond. George was from New
York and always talking that NY shit, you know like he was
so connected up there, but I knew he was faking about
something, I just couldn't put my hand on it. To me George
was a distraction to what we were doing with the music
and he never supported Rodney's music. When I sat down
in the chair by the balcony where the kitchen table was,
that's where the beat machine was. Rodney sat back
down on the couch beside George and kept playing
Madden. George looked over at me and with a big smile
said "Shit nigga, well you looking good" and we all laughed
and smiled. We talked for a few about jail and being back
home but I was ready to hear some beats. As I sat there
for a moment I felt that feeling of wanting this thing more
than Rodney. They continued to play for about twenty
minutes and then Rodney came over to the table with the
beat machine and played a beat. The beats Rodney played
were good and I had flow for days, but his set up was still
the same as before I went in to jail. He used samples a lot
and when the sample played on his beat machine he had

to manually hit the button for it to play. I was glad to be back in the presence of hearing new beats by Rodney but disappointed in that he hadn't invested in his equipment. Before I went in he was always saying, "Man if I had a MPC," which was short for Midi Production Center, that his beats would be tighter. What he had was alright, but he had his old drum machine hooked up to the house radio so everything was distorted. In order to put the beat on tape we would press record on the tape deck while he manually played the beat to make a cassette tape. This was a new day and I knew this type of way wasn't efficient to be the best, but Rodney was my man and I had faith we would grow with each other and run the game in D.C. one day.

After me and Rodney hooked up for the first time, we set up a meeting for us to make a team to start a movement that would get us known in the city. Rodney's friend Shamar was cool with us and he was Rodney's friend that also did beats. Shamar had a new drum machine that was more upgraded than Rodney's and his beats were tight. The only thing about Shamar was he was one those read a book, think he smart kind of cool cat swag ass nigga. A cold bitch for real, but we all tried to see the good in him. The fact about Shamar was that he always wanted to rap, and his raps were corny and we didn't want to tell him. Before I went in he would play his beats and each one I would like and I would start rapping to but, he would have a corny ass hook or something that just threw it off. Overlooking all that, Rodney and I said we would bring him in on the meeting. The only other person we considered to be in on this also was Rodney's old friend from District Heights named Shay. I knew Shay from when I stayed in Capital Heights. Shay was a lot older than me but I was down for it if it would make us better. So there it was, me and Rodney set up a meeting for all four of us at Rodney's apartment for the next week. Meanwhile, I also had my mind on finding my way in my hustle. I had mentioned to Rodney about trying to start my own clothing store, when I did he said, "My man Darrell got his own shop out Forestville, Maryland you should holler at him." So the next day I was on it and did just that. I found the store Rodney was talking about and stopped in there. I looked around and his custom clothing line was something I liked called Emage. There was an Asian guy behind the counter so as I looked around he asked me, "What's up man, what can I help you with?" With me just coming home from jail my attitude was up front and direct. I told him, "I like your stuff in here, how much would you charge me to buy your stuff at a price where I could sell it for my price in the street and make a profit?" The Asian guy eyes lit up like a candle and said "Ok look, my name Miles, give me a day, can you come back this time tomorrow?" I said, "Yes I could be here." He said, "Cool, come back tomorrow around this time and we can talk." I told him my name was Marc and I was a friend of someone Darell knows. He said cool we gone talk, and I left out the store with a feeling that I may have put myself in contact with the right people to help my vision. The next day, I returned to the store at the same time as discussed, and when I got there, Miles had a smile on his face from ear to ear and was all prepared for me. On the counter he had placed seven different shirts in stacks of five, and on the shirts where the fitted hats to match. Miles looked at me and said, "This all you," can you bring me back ten dollars for each shirt and six dollars for each hat? I was so amazed my heart pounded like a bass drum. I looked him in his eyes and said, "Yeah I got you." Miles then said, "I'm a write out an inventory list for all this, just sign it and it's yours." He wrote all the items out, I put them in a bag and left out immediately, no small talk, just to let him know my job started right then and it did. When I left the store with Miles, my first stop was over Rodney's house to fill him in on the good news. Once over Rodney's house, I brought in a few shirts and hats to show him what was up. Rodney looked at me with a smile on his face and said "That's what's up, Marc" and kept nodding his head like he was proud I had gone and done it. A few days went by and it was the day we all were meeting at Rodney's. I was there early kicking it with Rodney, then Shamar came in with Shay right on time. As they both came in, it was like a reunion, everybody smiling and nodding like yeah we're all here now. With no cut cards Rodney turned the TV off and we got to business. We all spoke one at a time and let everybody know what the plan was. Rodney and I already knew what we needed, this meeting was to get Shay and Shamar on the same page. We let Shamar know we needed him as a producer and let Shay know he needed to just do his thing as a rapper and be loyal to it. Both of them agreed to what we were trying to do and we went on with progress. Before the meeting was over, I said we need to come up with a name to stamp it. I wanted it to stand for the struggle, so as a unit together we came up with The Strugglaz. It was official after I said it, everyone loved it and it was on. We finished the meeting up and we all went our way for the night. When I left Rodney's I was motivated that we would do some damage together, Rodney and Shamar doing beats and me rapping with Shay doing his thing too. Now, in the back of my head we had all been around each other before I went to jail, but now for the sake of Rodney, everyone was trying to do it official. I knew Shay and Shamar had a tendency to bullshit and Rodney sometimes lacked the initiative to believe in himself. Rodney was my man, his beats were hot, that's why we called him Hot Rodd, but this nigga never invested in getting better equipment to compete with industry production. The thing was though, every day he had a bag of weed to smoke or found a way to get high. A few months went by and it was the same old shit, just a different toilet. Shamar was always adding a negative vibe to the group and never wanted to really let me get a beat from him, and Shay was still doing his own disloyal outside business. Shay never could write to any of the beats, he would love to come over, get high and drunk and freestyle over the beats they played. Freestyling is cool and all, but he lacked the focus to write a rap down and make a real song. Then Shays disloyalty became evident. He would freestyle at our meetings and always say his name was Shystalinee, so we finally stopped him one day and Shamar and Rodney was like "Shay, if Shyst is Shyst, you can't be called Shystalinee." We all shook our heads in disbelief because he really admired me that much where he wanted to be called Shystalinee. Even though they took it lightly, I thought it was the ultimate betrayal of a rapper who took my inspiration and tried to make a name for himself. Shay used to be out around Forest Creek, on the Maryland side. So one day, I stopped through on him to see what's up and as we were talking in the parking lot where everyone hustled at, a little youngin came up to him and was like "Hey, Shyst." When the boy called him that, Shay's eyes got big like golf balls and kind of shook his head as to say, no. I acted like I didn't hear it, but I heard it clear enough to let Rodney and them know he was a lame for that shit, and I didn't want him coming around me anymore.

Now all-in-all, I had been doing well in the streets with selling clothes out my trunk with Elmage. I was going back and forth out of town in VA and had clientele in D.C. and Maryland with it. I had hustled my way to a bubble crown victoria with the police package in it. I wasn't rich but I was doing well in the streets. One day I just had enough, it was evident that Rodney wanted to play madden with his man George and my effort to make it with them was a waste of time for the time being and I prayed to God for a better opportunity.

Stepping away from Rodney wasn't easy at all because at the time it was all I knew, but I still had my hustle with my clothes and I was pumping. I had everything: sweat suits, jackets, all type of female skirts and all. Miles and Darrell were cool at Emage because they knew about my music and even Darrell was always plugging me in with what he could help me out with. By this time I was even working in the store in Forestville. The experience in the store was what I really wanted. I didn't get paid to be there I just did what was needed to get the store right. The designers of Emage, Vic and Everton created and did the sewing in the back of the. Vic was a hood nigga, and Everton was a Jamaican. They kept it one hundred with me all the time and used to have me laughing throughout the day. When fine girls would come in the store, they would do stuff like, come from the back and say, "You know I got a new dress I need someone to try on" and it would work. The women would change and come out in one of their dresses and look amazing. They were vicious with their style. They would make shirts and sweat suit blanks for other urban clothing lines also in there, but when they didn't come and get their orders, they would let me buy them. With access to my own designers, I started my own clothing line called Struggle Life Wear. The one thing I had the upper hand with was that I was in the street so I knew what the people wanted and I made the adjustments and request they were looking for.

Two weeks had gone by and I had managed to stop going by Rodney's place. I switched my focus and was on my grind, I was coming back from out of town in VA and I stopped in Waldorf, Maryland at St. Charles Mall. While I was in there, I bumped into a longtime friend of mine that I knew from VA named Poppy. Poppy told me he was rapping now and knew I got busy on the mic and invited *me to come pass his studio one day to get on a track with him. I agreed to hook up with him, so we switched numbers and went our way. That night at home I thought about when I bumped into Poppy and then I thought about what I was going through, so I said, "Fuck it," I need to keep moving forward and see what's good. The next day, I hit Poppy up like, "What's good cuz?" He said he had to hit the studio tomorrow and if I wanted, I could come through. I was like, "Bet, what time?" He told me in the evening at about four o'clock but to come when I could because he and Frank would be at his house writing. Frank was another old friend of mine I knew from hanging out in VA, real good dude, I just never knew he rapped. The next day, I left my apartment in D.C. and got down to Waldorf about two o'clock. When I got to Poppy's house, he came out to get me with a big smile on his face. Poppy was one of them crazy looking dudes who looked up to no good if you didn't know him, but when he smiled, he could brighten up a room. Poppy stayed with his mom because he was still young, about nineteen or twenty. We came in through the back door, walked through the kitchen and went upstairs to his room. Once in his room, he played a beat on his* computer and pulled out his pad. Poppy had a bunk bed set up but the bottom was a layout couch. I sat down and when he turned up the volume on the computer the beat was stupid crazy. I was like, "Damn, who beat is that?" Poppy looked at me through the corner of his eye and smiled at me and said, "This the joint we recording today. Frank on his way now". I sat back while he played his beat thinking this beat crazy, then I asked him "Who did this joint" and he said, "The dudes who studio we record at, they're producers". I nodded and said, "Ok, they tight." I was impressed by the sound and just was happy to hear some new beats. We sat there for about twenty minutes and then Frank came through. Frank came straight in the room like he lived there, and said, "Shyst, what up Shyst?" I stood up, dapped him up and we all talked for a bit and then I let them write. About an hour went by and we left out to head to the studio where they recorded. They hopped in the car with each other and I followed behind them. It took us about ten minutes to get there, then we pulled into these commercial type buildings and I figured this was it. Once we got out the car, I could hear music in the inside. As I listened, I heard a cranking beat playing loud enough to know that this joint was official. As we walked in the studio there was a sign on the door that said City Vibe Records as we came in and that's when they introduced me to their producers, a set of twins named Anton and Anthony. When they stood to speak to me they stood about 6'2 and were identical, they both greeted me and then sat down to work with Frank and Poppy. They introduced me as Marc who raps. After that, I sat down on the couch to see how they conducted their session, being as though this was my first time inside an official studio since I got out of jail. I noticed how Frank and Poppy interacted with each other. They were more like the joking type with each other, sort of like a real live two Stooges, and that's not to disrespect them but to give a picture on the back and forth play arguing and fighting with each other they did. While observing the studio an older guy came in, he was heavy set and short, he had a hat on his head that kind of covered his eyes and everyone yelled, "What's up, pops?" I greeted him and sat back down. Pops was the father of Anton and Anthony and he just referred to them as the twins. By this time Anton was sitting in front of the mixing board and asked Frank and

Poppy, "You all write to the Joint?" They both replied, "Yea, we ready." Anton played the beat on the big studio monitors. The beat played as they pulled out the pads, Frank and Poppy both were from Virginia, so the name of their group together was called VA Slims. The name fit them perfectly and with Anton and Anthony producing them, they had a good sound. While they set up to record the song they were working on, I was like a kid in a candy store with no money, excited to be there and eager to work. Anton set up the microphone in the booth and they started recording, the song was called VA Slims. Back at that time I used to smoke Black & Mild cigars. I asked them, "Is it cool to smoke my black out front?" Anthony nodded speedily like yeah, so when I stepped out front to light my cigar up, Anthony followed out to smoke a cigarette. Once we were outside, I lit my black up and Anthony lit his cigarette. First question Anthony asked me was, "Where you from man?" I told him I was from D.C., the northeast part. Then he asked me, "So you rap?" I replied to him, "Yeah, I get down." He said, "That's what's up man, let me hear something one day". I told him I had been in the studio awhile back but I was trying to get back in soon. While we conversed in front, the music from the session inside was rumbling to the outside, a sound that was oh so good to my ears because it meant that work was going on. I asked Anthony, "You do beats too?" He told me, "Yea, my brother Anton had been doing it for about five years and I just got serious about doing beats about two years ago". He continued to tell me that he and his brother were called Manistyles, because their sound was so versatile, they could do all kind of beats. He asked me if I had anything on cd he could hear, I let him know I had something on tape I could let him hear because that's all I had. I walked to my car, got the tape out of my compartment, it was something I had done with Rodney prior to me going to jail. As I gave it to him I let him know that the producer that I did it with had a small drum machine and we did what we could with what we had. Anthony was cool though, he said, "It's cool though, we started out the same way man." I was kind of embarrassed a little but Anthony seemed excited to hear what I could do. While we were talking his brother Anton came out with sort of a serious look on his face and let Anthony know they were almost done. We went back in

- 62 -

the studio to hear the finished product of the song they were recording. Anton hit play and the beat came on, he turned the volume up, it seemed on blast, the joint came on and sounded good. While it was playing, Anton was doing a rough mix to the track, which enhanced the sound quality of the song. Frank and Poppy both were nodding as I was too. I was proud of them for nailing this joint, because it was inspiring me. When the song ended, Anton looked at Frank and Poppy and was like, "All right we got about three more to do then we should have enough." As they talked it was clear they were working on a CD to put out. They wrapped up the session and we all started heading out to the front. As we departed I told Anton, Anthony and Pops nice meeting them and hope to see them soon, they said the same as Frank, Poppy and I walked to our cars. Before pulling off, we stood in the parking lot as they played the CD in the car of the song they just recorded. I told Poppy I appreciated this session and how proud of them I was. I told him we about to kill this shit when I get in the studio and put some songs down. They agreed, we talked for a minute and Poppy said, "I'll hit you tomorrow Shyst,so you can come back when we record again." When I pulled off and got on the highway to get back home, I felt uplifted. Being in the studio that night was what I needed, and it gave me hope to get to where I was trying to go when I came home from jail. When I got home I let my family know about the session I was at and the new hope I had found with these new producers. In my prayers that night I had to thank God for hearing my prayers and giving me new light in my life. My clothing hustle was good and all I wanted now was to work in the studio and drop a record. I went back to the studio a few days later with Frank and Poppy to support their CD. The next time I went back, Anthony let me know that the tape I had left him was good as far as my rapping. He laughed a little and said, "Just the quality of the beat was off". Again, it embarrassed me a little, but Anthony was like, "It is cool though bro we going to work with you and get you tight." Once he said that it was like hitting the lottery because I knew with my style and their beats I could kill it. After that day I was at the studio with Frank and Poppy every day for the next few weeks while they finished their CD titled VA Slims. Frank and Poppy were mediocre artists, but they played constantly, and they sometimes took for granted the opportunity that Manistyles and City Vibe was giving them. Frank and Poppy's rap style was sort of fictional, as where they didn't rap about the street or anything, they just fantasized and rapped about themselves as big named artist's in the game; something they were far from. Once their CD was complete, the twins took pictures for them and printed their CD to push in the streets, this was something that I had never seen done, much less anyone give an artist that much support to help them do it. When it came to Manistyles as a production team and City Vibe as a business, Anton took on the role of keeping things tight. Anthony stayed chill until it got out of hand and things got serious to where there was no money being made and their rent for the building was due. There were times that I could tell that Frank and Poppy's playing and arguing with each other became too much for the studio. The twins recorded other artist's but this CD for Frank and Poppy was their way of getting their production out and hopefully get them a deal. Once the CD was finished and printed up, it was time for Frank and Poppy to hit the streets to sell themselves. I supported them so much that when it was done I took some of their CD's to help sell them to people I knew. City Vibe printed about one hundred CD's for them to start out with, I took like twenty of them to help them out and to show my support. The CD had dope beats and production on it, but I was in the street and all I knew were hustlers, from D.C., Maryland and Virginia, I basically ran the streets. I sold all twenty of them while grinding with my clothes too, so they went like nothing to me. Everyone I sold it to said it was alright, but wondered where my CD was, and that's what I got from everyone that bought it. I knew why, it just didn't catch their ears. After a few weeks Frank and Poppy's playing started to become aggravating to Manistyles because they had only moved about thirty CD's between the two of them and I moved twenty by myself. The twins saw my ambition to hustle and that's what caught their attention. By this time, I was stopping by the studio on my own and had built a good relationship with Anton and Anthony. When I sold all out of Frank and Poppy's CD, the twins wanted to see if I could move more CD's since they needed the money. I had to be honest with them and tell them that it was kind of hard to keep selling to my clientele because I was in the city of D.C in the streets. I let them know it was sort of like selling vegetables in a bakery, I just needed the right product and I could move numbers. So we sat down and put together a plan, they would put a demo together for me of three songs to see what it would do. I agreed to split the sales of the CD's to bring money to the studio to help them out financially. Anton and Anthony told me to come back in two days and they would have some beats for me. During those two days I went to church that Sunday and stayed focused. The thing about me was, although I was in the street, from the time I left jail, I always stayed spiritually grounded. God was my strength and my power, my spiritual side is what the twins liked the most about me. In our conversations, Anthony and Anton both told me that when they were about five years old, a woman prophesied on them and said they would be musicians, this was before they ever picked up an instrument. I loved that, and I knew I had a purpose with them.

After two days went by, I called Anton at the studio and asked if he was ready for me. He said, "Yeah," he got something for me and to be down there about five o clock. When it got about four o'clock, I broke through traffic like

*a river rushing in a flood to get to the studio to see what
was up. When I got to the studio, Anton and Anthony was
there working on beats. When I came in Anton said,
"Shyst", in excitement and was smiling from ear-to-ear. I
was eager to hear what they had for me. Anton turned to
the computer and said, "What you think of this?" When he
pressed play, the beat came on and was crazy! It was a
bounce beat with a Timbaland edge, something that Frank
and Poppy could never do because this joint was serious.
While the beat played, I was bouncing like I could hear
words on it already. I told him, "I love this joint, it's crazy!"
Anton turned it down and said, "Cool, I'm going to burn
this one, take it and write to it and let's see how it comes
out." Once he burned it, I stayed for a few minutes and left
to go home to start writing. When I got in my car, I
popped the beat in my CD deck and let it play all the way
home. I knew in my heart I was going to make a banger
and it was like waiting for Christmas to get back to record.
I got home that night, wrote to the beat and was back the
next day to record. All my patience and support had all
added up to this moment. I went in the booth and
delivered. What came out was a premature hit called,*

"When and How", a song for females about getting intimate however we could. It was a smash to me. When he played it back loud, everyone in the studio was bouncing. When we finished, Anton gave me a CD that had two more beats on it and told me, "When you come up with something to these two hit me." I agreed and he burned my new song on CD and I left to finish the two new beats I just had got from them. I played "When and How" so many times over the next few days that I'm surprised it didn't wear out the CD. The other two beats were a different style than all the types I had heard on Frank and Poppy's CD. I liked the fact they made them just for me. Over the next two days I stayed focused on writing to the two beats, and after two days I was done. The day after I finished writing, I hit Anton again to set the studio time up for the following day. When I got to the studio, to record it was business as usual. This time, I invited Frank and Poppy by to sit in on the session. They both came through to support, but this time their demeanor wasn't as playful, they didn't seem mad but I could tell they were a little in their feelings. I hit the booth and killed both beats. What came out was a song called, "Too Hot," a song about the

street life and, "My Demons," a spiritual song about temptations. Anton and Anthony were both excited about how they came out, more or less they liked my creativity and my subject matter. Up to this point, the fairytale style of Frank and Poppy had blocked their vision of something real. When the session was over we all sat down together: me, the VA Slims and the twins.

Since I had now finished my demo and Frank and Poppy had the VA Slims CD out, we all needed to see how we could sell these CD's and get our name out in the streets. Me, already having my network together with my clothes, I had an idea of us doing a show in VA where Frank and Poppy were from. I had a lot of family on that side too, who wanted to see me perform. So, I knew it would be a winner. Anthony and Anton agreed and so did Frank and Poppy. I told everyone I had a building that I could get in Virginia that would be a good spot to do it. We all left the studio that night with one thing as our focus, sell CD's. The next day I made some calls to get the building reserved and I locked in a date. When I called the studio the next day to let the twins know I had the building, Anthony answered and told me to come down so we could put it together. When I got there, we kicked it about the show and then they played me the mixed version of my new songs. The mix on the three songs were on point, the levels were straight and I sounded like a professional. While they were playing the songs, I was in another world, a world I used to think about in jail and now I was here. When the songs finished playing, Anton looked at me and said, "We done, Shyst," with a smile on his face. This was my first demo and I couldn't wait to get it to the streets. Over the next few days, the twins worked on my artwork and putting my demo together, while I got things straight for the show. I locked the date for the following month, and it was a go. The only thing left for me and the VA Slims to do was promote it. When the CD's were ready, I stopped by the studio and they had printed up one hundred CD's just as they had done with the VA Slims. I took fifty out the door and they were gone in a week, I sold them for seven dollars and split the money with the studio. Anton and Anthony were so impressed with my hustle it brought us closer as friends. Meanwhile, Frank and Poppy collectively had still only sold about thirty CD's. Frank and Poppy were my dudes, but business-wise, they didn't take what was at hand seriously. The twins knew I was on point and it motivated them to help me more. There were only a few weeks left until the show and I had already sold my one hundred CDs out the trunk. The twins started putting together another load for me for the show because I had a lot of people coming. During the time leading to the show, Frank and Poppy kind of faded off from being around the studio as much, and I was there even more because our business was booming. I had the streets jumping, people the twins knew where interested in me, even investors wanted to put up money to further my music. The day of the show had finally arrived, I had been promoting all month, and by this time I was on my second batch of one hundred CDs. I had posters and flyers printed at Kinkos to have in the building where we were performing. With all my materials in place, we met at the studio around three o' clock, since it was about a two-hour ride to Virginia where the venue was located. Frank and Poppy showed up on time, but their energy was off, they weren't playing anymore and their relationship with the twins wasn't the same as it used to be. I think they took it more personal than understanding the business at hand. I wasn't tripping about them though because honestly, they had a chance to shine and I know how it goes in the street when jealousy comes. They had enough respect to keep cool with me because, outside of rap, they knew I got busy in the streets on a level they knew nothing about. We rolled out to the show, three cars deep and got there at the scheduled time. The building was an old elementary school in Farnham, Virginia named Julia G Page. They had a lot of parties there and it was perfect for us to bring our own crowd. All of my supporters that purchased my demo was there. As I began to set up it was looking good, people were starting to turn out and come in. As we were about to start the show, you could see Frank and Poppy had done no promotion and had no supporters there, only those who knew them because of me. Their demeanor that night was distant, they were spoiled to the grind and didn't know how to interact as performers. Being though everyone was there for me, I let them open up and I finished it off and killed the show, selling the remainder of my CD's there and having a great performance out of town in Virginia. The night was a success for me and the twins. This was only the beginning of what we were going to do together.

CHAPTER 5

TEST OF FAITH

(Hebrews 11:1)

Faith is the substance of things hoped for, and the evidence of things not seen.

After the show in Virginia, Anton, Anthony, and I became even closer as friends, almost as brothers. As the weeks went by I would go to church on Sundays to feed my spirit, as I did in jail. That's what kept me on point with life situations around me. Being as though I had done my first show in VA, I was still pushing my demo in the streets and trying to get it out to everyone I could. At the time in D.C. the number one radio station, 95.5 FM had what they called, "D.C. Home Jams," on Sunday nights. That's when they would play the best local artist's music in the city if it got approved by the station and by Dj Flexx. My demo was hot and I wanted to see if it could make the cut, so I got the address, got up enough courage, and sent it in for a try. I figured it was worth the attempt. Meanwhile, things at City Vibe Studios were growing for them, with VA Slims

CD slightly moving around and my demo floating in the streets, a lot of local artists who knew the twins prior, had started coming through and recording. The thing I loved about the twins was that they were loyal to me as their artist. They recorded other artist and groups, but I was their artist specifically. They would promote me as such to everyone, this made a lot of artists admire me, and want to work with me or get a verse from me on their songs. At times I would write songs and hooks for a few local artists who wanted my help, but the twins kept me grounded and would stay focused on getting me better by keeping me in the studio working on songs. About two weeks went by from the time I sent my demo into the radio station. I was eager to know if they had received my CD and if it would be played. I called up to the station and kept getting a busy signal, I kept calling until it finally went through. The phone rang so long that I got irritated and was about to hang up. Right at that moment, someone answered, they picked up and said, "WPGC, this Dj Flexx. What's up?" I couldn't believe it! "Flexx, its Marc Shyst." I sent my demo in, a song called, "When and how?" Did ya'll get it? In an excited voice, he was like, "Yeah homie we got it, that joint is going to play this Sunday." I told him, "All right cool, thank you Flexx." I hung up and was so amped up that I damn near fell on the floor from jumping around. My heart was beating as if someone had told me I won the lottery. Then, I got right back on the phone and hit the twins at the studio to tell them the good news. They were happy for me, but even they couldn't know how much this meant to me, it was everything to me. All my hard work was about to be heard live on the radio. I called everyone I knew and told them to listen in on Sunday because my song was going to be played. A few days went by and Sunday was finally upon us. I was out of town in Virginia that weekend and headed back home that day. My Aunt, Doretha that lived in Philly was in town visiting that weekend. My mom called me and asked me if I could bring her back up to D.C. with me, so she could catch the train back to Philly. I told her yea, so by the time I caught up with Aunt Doretha it was nearly eight o'clock that night. DC Home Jams came on at nine, so I was racing to get across the border to Maryland so my radio could pick up 95.5. The station wouldn't pick up in Virginia where we were. So with my sister, Theresa in the front seat, she came back with me and my Aunt Doretha in the back seat, we were all anticipating my song being played on the radio. As it neared about ten minutes to nine, I was just getting over the border of Maryland leaving out of Virginia. I turned the station to 95.5, a little static could be heard, but it was on and that was all that mattered. When Dj Flexx came on and started DC Home Jams at nine o'clock, I was as nervous as a cat locked in a doghouse waiting to see if he played my song or not. Dj Flexx played two local artists songs, I started to get a little anxious thinking it wouldn't play, and then Dj Flexx came on and said, "I like this next joint, it's called When and How by Marc Shyst, on WPGC 95.5 Home Jams." When the song came on we were all hollering so much in the car I couldn't even hear the song. As the song played my voice broke through the speakers like I had a record deal. I was bouncing up and down so much the car was rocking. I looked back at my Aunt Doretha who at the time was in her fifty's and even she was bouncing around with joy. When the song finished playing we were all out of breath like we just got off a roller coaster. My Aunt Doretha said, "That was good baby, I know you going to make it big."

When she said that it really uplifted me because she was really spiritual, and I knew she believed it. While on the highway headed back to D.C. I had to pass by the studio in Waldorf, I told my sister and aunt I had to stop for a minute. When I got out of the car, I had my chest out and a smile on my face like I just beat Mike Tyson. I walked in the studio and the twins were all smiles as I said, "You hear the joint?" they replied, "Yea we heard it." Pops was there too and with a smile on his face, laughing, he said, "That joint rocked!" We all were happy. There was so much commotion as if it were a football game on. I told them I was coming back from VA, had my people waiting in the car and that I would be back tomorrow. They all said, "Alright" and congratulated me and I left out. When the news spread to everyone who recorded at City Vibe, all the artists who came by looked at me like the golden boy. With my song being played on the radio and with an out-of-town show under our belt, we put together a plan to do more shows locally, around D.C., and Maryland. A lot of artists who heard me would, "He sounds like 50 Cent," who is an artist out of New York who was blowing up in the hip hop game. I always felt like the people who said it were *trying to discredit why my music was good. I used to let it*

motivate me to keep making great records. One of the

artists who started recognizing me at the studio was an

artist by the name of Vuki Mukud. Vuki was from South

Africa and had a clothing line in Maryland. When Vuki

started recording there, he was so arrogant that he would

walk by me and not even speak. Vuki had a lot of

awareness in D.C. for his clothing line and he used it to

manipulate radio Dj's and even my producers, by giving

them free clothes for favors. To me, he was a fake and a

wannabe, who always talked about Jay- Z this and Jay- Z

that. He listened to Jay-Z so much that he tried to mimic

his style in his raps. The thing about Vuki was he was from

South Africa and wanted to act like he was from D.C., he

never wanted where he was truly from to be known. I

always looked at him as a fraud for that. The twins

couldn't stand to record him because he would take five

hours literally to do one song. He could never rap a whole

line without stopping and going back. He was fooling a lot

of people so much that even his clothing line was a fluke. I

found out he was going to New York buying clothes,

wholesale, and just switching the tags like it was his line. I couldn't stand this dude, but I humbled myself because at the time, I was heavy in my bible and his demeanor was everything God was telling me about men, these last days and as such waited patiently on the Lord to expose him. With my new song hitting the radio and all the attention coming my way, it forced Vuki to recognize me. When he would come to the studio, he even had his man Dwight who was a good dude asks me to be down with them. I denied him and told him, "I'm all right." "I'll be around though for you if you need me for anything." That's how much I was buzzing in D.C. at this point. All the riff-raff finally came in the open about Vuki though. The twins had set up a show for me in Waldorf at this new club called Icons. Icons was a new spot that just opened were a lot of people would be there on the weekends. So the twins talked with the owner and they let me come down on a Saturday and to perform. I guess the news was heard by Vuki because the day of the show, we all met up at the club and he showed up. I knew something was up because he came by himself. Vuki was the scared type who always kept someone or a group with him. My red flag went up when I saw him pop up alone. When he came in I asked

Anthony, "What is he doing here?" He smiled and said,
"Oh, we told him he could perform, he just going to open
up for you." That was cool with me, but nobody saw him
perform, so we were all curious about what he was going
to do. The club was packed, it had to be about four
hundred people there and it was time to go on. As we
were about to perform, we all hit the stage and prepped
the Dj to play our songs. It was time, they gave Vuki the
mic and his beat came on, the beat was produced by the
twins, so when it played the crowd was nodding
anticipating hearing a rap. As the beat played for nearly
ten seconds Vuki started rapping, he said his first line and
forgot his words to the song. When he messed up in front
of everyone, he looked at the Dj and said, "Hold up hold up,
run it back." The Dj rewinded the track and the beat
started again. As the beat played all eyes were on him like
a fish in a tank. He started rapping again, said his first line
and forgot his words again. This time it was embarrassing
to us, the crowd had frowns and people started talking
about him amongst themselves. This fool looks at the Dj
and says, "One more time, one more time." Everyone in
the crowd was like, "Oh no!" The Dj started playing the

beat over again and just like an old TV episode, this joker forgot his words. This time when he forgot his words, he was so embarrassed himself, he looked at the crowd spoke in the microphone and said, "Sike y'all I don't really rap, I'm here for my man." As he brought me the microphone I was so disgusted with him because by now the crowd was all in an uproar to the point of booing him. I looked at him, shook my head, and got the crowd back in order. The Dj played my beat and as everyone stared at me thinking I would fold, I rocked the whole spot. I turned the stage out, people were dancing so hard that I had two ladies come on stage and dance while I was rapping. Because Vuki's performance was so bad it was almost like I was the savior of the night. When I came off stage people were high fiving me and giving me handshakes as they complimented me. I stayed around until the club was over and the twins even sold a few of my CD's while we posted at our table. Before the night was over mysteriously Vuki disappeared and was nowhere to be found. When the show was over we went back to the studio, kicked it for a while and I went home. That night was only the beginning for me though with Vuki. I knew he wasn't solid and his embarrassment at my performance was enough for me. I wanted to expose him for the undercover fraud he was, but his embarrassment to himself that night was what I knew he had in him. The news of my performance spread in the streets like wildfire and every artist that knew the twins wanted me to be on their show with them because of my following. My following was even bringing me other artists that heard of me the ability to trust me to write for them, one artist in particular that I met there was named Sofi Green. Sofi had the look of a star and needed help putting together a few songs. We worked well with each other and stayed friends ever since.

There was a group of rock and roll rappers that use to record at City Vibe by the name of Rigamortiz. They were four white boys that rapped to rock and roll type of production. Rigamortiz knew all about me from hearing my songs at the studio and the buzz of my shows. One day while at the studio, I had the chance to meet them for the first time. They embraced me like I had a record deal, they were true fans of my music, and when I heard their music we had mutual respect. About a month went by after my initial introduction to Rigamortiz and Anton called me up and said: "Yo you down to do a show with Rigamortiz?" I was like "Cool", so Aton told me it was in Baltimore in April at a club called The Depot. I had done a few talents shows in Baltimore some years back, but nothing to this extent. Rigamortiz had a following of their own and they wanted me to be their opener. My birthday was in April, so to me, I thought what better way to celebrate early than to do a show in Baltimore. With a show in Baltimore coming up, I also managed to book me a show in D.C. with a promoter called Double O Productions at a well-known club called 2K9. The Baltimore show was on a Friday and my show in D.C. at 2K9 was on that following Sunday, so it worked out perfectly and I was able to do both. The week of my shows was truly hectic, with moving in the street with clothes and getting two show CD's ready for the weekend, I felt like I was in the industry for real. I was so happy because I was living the life I dreamed of and it was my reality. To top things off, the week of my show a good friend of Pops and the twins named Mr. Randall, who was an investor had an opportunity for me. He had a slot for an opening act in New York opening up for Ludacris, Busta Rhymes, Jada kiss, and a few other acts at Nassau Coliseum. That show was scheduled for the week after we were in Baltimore and D.C. Now with this show on the schedule, we were at the top of our game and it couldn't get any better.

It was finally the Friday of the show in Baltimore and the twins and I were all ready and pumped for it. I met them at City Vibe, as we had normally done before a show and they got in with me and I drove up to Baltimore to the Depot for my show. Once we got to the club, you could hear the music outside of the club pouring out to the street. As we walked in I was anticipating anything and it was more than I could imagine. When I stepped in, I looked and saw the members of Rigamortiz at the bar sitting down. So the twins and I walked over, and we all shook hands with smiles of joy. Rigamortiz was excited that I came through for them and the kept saying, "Shyst man we appreciate this man." I let them know it was no problem and my pleasure. As I got settled in at the club, I looked over to the dance floor and saw there was a band playing on stage. Now I've seen rock and roll bands play live before, but this was different. They were in a mosh pit going crazy. The crowd was jumping up and down pushing and shoving each other in all joy and happiness like they *had all gone crazy. As I stood there in aww with a Kool-Aid smile on my face, a white boy jumping up and down bounced over to me and put his sweaty forehead on my forehead lightly and said: "Come on bro get in." I looked in amazement and literally broke out in laughter. The energy was crazy in there and I was digging it. It was finally my time to go on and I was ready. I was the only hip hop rapper there and I wanted to give them what they didn't expect. As I set up to go on, people start filling the floor, I introduced myself to the crowd, said a few words of peace and respect and got to it. When I was performing the crowd was hype, I mean they were all rock and roll heads partying to my music. The show got crazy when two girls who were in the front row as I performed started kissing each other right there on the dance floor. When I came off stage from performing the whole club gave me a round of applause. What followed after that was a new dimension for me. This wasn't my first show, but this was the first time I truly felt like a star. As I sat down near the bar I remember people approaching me all night with compliments, I can remember a guy who asked me was I good and did I want a drink? I said "Yeah, what's your* name?" and he said "Matt" and I downed the drink like water while almost finishing the first drink he bought, he looked at me again and said: "You need another?" With me celebrating at the moment I paused and agreed "Yea John" and we busted out laughing and he said "It's Matt", being this was like the third time I asked his name. When I finished the last drink I was done. The alcohol had intoxicated me so much that my legs had a mind of their own. So the twins and I made our way out the club. As I went to walk down the stairs I realized how much I couldn't control myself. I held on to the rail, made my way out the club, and staggered to my car. At this point, driving us home was out the question, so I let Anton drive while Anthony was in the front. I sat in the back to gather myself together and hopefully sober up while driving home, I couldn't stay awake and passed out from drunkenness. I woke up at one point feeling sick, I hollered to Anthony "Pullover a bra, pull over." Anthony pulled on the side of the road and I opened the back door, leaned my head out, and vomited. I pulled myself back in my car, closed the door, and we pulled off driving again. I passed out again, only to wake up with the same vomiting feeling, I yelled out again and he pulled over and I threw up again. I pulled myself back in and passed back out. Once we got to the studio, I was in no condition to drive, so the twins told me to come in and rest until I could drive home. That rest turned into the next morning. When I woke up in the studio it had to be about nine a.m. in the morning. I woke up to my stomach feeling ill, so I hurried to the bathroom and threw up again. Once I got myself together I looked around the studio and the twins were knocked out sleep, so I grabbed my keys from off the table and left to head home. Once on the highway the ill feeling in my stomach continued, it was so bad that I pulled over twice to throw up before I reached home. When I got home, I immediately got in bed hoping the sickness would leave my body. Later that evening I was awakened to a phone call from my mother asking me if I wanted to go out to eat with my family to celebrate my birthday. I agreed and woke out of my sleep to get dressed and left out to celebrate over dinner. At this time I was feeling ok and the pain in my stomach was slightly gone, so my family and I met at a restaurant called Jaspers and had dinner. When I left the restaurant I returned back home to lay down.

What followed that night was a very intense pain that came back to my stomach. I truly had no idea what it could have been, so I sucked it up and laid down hoping it would go away. When I woke up Sunday morning the pain had intensified with me vomiting again. After I threw up a few times I was in so much pain I couldn't leave my bathroom. I laid on the floor and remained there for hours unable to move. I eventually gathered enough strength to make it to my phone to call my mother who stayed across the street from me, told her I wasn't feeling well, and it may be food poison. When she knocked at my door I had to crawl to get there and open it. When she came in and seen my condition she looked at me like she could tell I was in severe pain, she screamed: "You want to go to the hospital." I told her, yeah but I couldn't get up to make it there, she then said in a panicking voice, "You want me to call an ambulance." The thought of an ambulance scared me, so I quickly said "No." I grabbed my jacket and with the help of my mom made it to the emergency room at Prince Georges Hospital. Once I got in the emergency room I limped to the seat and sat down while my mother filled out my paperwork, I was in so much pain I literally was laying out in the chair. Later my girlfriend at the time came to the hospital while we waited for me to be seen. Sitting in the waiting room the pain in my stomach became so intense that it was now unbearable. The waiting room was packed with patients waiting to be seen, there were so many that I knew it would be an hour or more before I was going to be seen by a doctor. As I observed patients coming in, you either had to be shot, stabbed, or out of consciousness to be seen immediately. After waiting for almost an hour I couldn't take it anymore and I put my plan into work, I told my family I couldn't wait anymore, I got up, walked through the double doors to the back, and literally fell out in the floor. When I hit the ground, what followed was a rush of nurses to aide me and they put me on a stretcher. Once I was on the stretcher, the nurses pulled my chart and started assessing me immediately. I told them I was in deep pain and they asked: "On a level of one to ten, how bad is the pain?" I told them twelve and they gave me pain medicine that was so strong it knocked me out. What followed after that was a blur of events that seemed to happen in a few hours, but lasted all day. I first awoke in a waiting room in a doctor's office laying in an examination chair. As I woke up, I looked to the right of me, my girlfriend was there looking at me in deep concern, I asked her where was I, and she said in a check-in room. By this time they had drawn blood and were doing tests on me. About twenty minutes went by, a male doctor who looked to be from India came in, and said, "Mr.Ball we have to run some test on your stomach to see what's wrong, ok," I agreed to him, he then handed me a twelve-ounce cup of what seemed to be water, and said "I need you to drink this, so we can see what's in your stomach Mr.Ball." I took the cup from him, as he left I smelled the liquid, and it smelled like vanilla, I held my breath and gulped it down as if it tasted like sour milk. I then closed my eyes and the next time I woke up; I was in an examination room with what seemed to be a time portal machine. This machine looked like something off the TV and not real. The nurses lifted me off the stretcher and laid me on a flat table. When they laid me on the table a big machine started turning, the table slid me inside of it, and examined my stomach to see what was wrong with me. I stayed awake the whole time this machine was examining me because truthfully this machine had me *thinking some old science fiction stuff like I was about to*

be cloned. When they were done testing, I was wheeled

back into another room. This room was a little smaller

than the first room and it only had a curtain for privacy. I

was later joined by my family in the room I was taken to. I

still was in pain a little, so I fell back to sleep again from

the medication I had taken. I later woke up to a nurse in

my room saying that I was going to have to have surgery in

order to help me get better, she handed me a chart pad

that had a paper on it. She told me that I needed to sign

the paper to confirm that if anything went wrong in

surgery that the hospital wasn't at fault. When she

handed it to me I just stared at it as I was reading it, she

then said, "I'll be back in a few to get it," I said ok, and as

she left out the room my girlfriend at the time looked at

me with fear and said "You going to sign it?" When she

said that it really angered me because I wasn't in any

position not to sign it. My thought then in my head was

like, what am I supposed to not sign it and die. I looked at

her, just took a deep sigh, without saying anything, and

with no hesitation signed the form. When I signed it I put

all my trust in the Lord that I would be ok and make it

through this. Everything seemed to be happening so fast that I couldn't keep track of what time it was and which day of the week it was at this point. I fell back to sleep and the next time I awoke I was in a room in the hospital in an open space with an Asian nurse sitting next to me. When I looked over at her, I asked her where I was, she stated I was being prepped for surgery. When she said that I had the feeling of getting on a roller coaster that you have waited in line for, you really want to turn around and get out of line. Just then she was checking my arms and vitals, she reached down to my pubic area and grabbed my penis, I yelled out "Hold up lady, what are you doing?" She said, "I have to put a catheter in you for surgery Mr. Ball." I said "A catheter," she then let me know it's for me to use the bathroom during surgery. I couldn't believe it, I mean the surgery was one thing, but this was ridiculous to me. She proceeded to grab my penis and insert a tube through my penis, as she pushed it in, I screamed as if I were being stung by ten hornets. "Ahhhhh" I screamed as she kept pushing the tube all the way to my bladder, once it hit my bladder, she stopped I then took a deep breath, shook my head, and just laid back on the stretcher awaiting surgery.

About thirty minutes went by, a transporter came, and wheeled me out to surgery. As I was being wheeled to surgery I was in the state of mind of heading to my funeral and the day of my birth. When I got in the surgery room we entered through two metal doors and two doctors along with about six nurses were all waiting for me. As they were about to put me on the operating table, something was wrong because one of the doctors started telling the nurses that he wasn't prepped properly. As they lifted my body I was still hooked to IV's on the stretcher, so when they went to place me on the operating table my body was jerked back to the stretcher. At this point, I was in fear because in the back of my mind I was like "These people don't know what they're doing." They laid me on the operating table, I looked up to a big operating light over me and then it was just like I saw in the movies. A nurse leaned over to me, placed the anesthesia mask over my mouth, and said, "Mr. Ball take a deep breath for me," I took a deep breath and once I inhaled the first breath and exhaled out. I closed my eyes and fell into another world of darkness, how long I was there, I don't know, what the doctors were doing to me, I had no idea. The only thing I knew was the place I was in gave me peace from the world and freed me of this pain. The next time I slightly woke to crack my eyes, I was back in the recovery room. When I attempted to open my eyes fully, I couldn't. I peeped over to my right and there was the same Asian lady beside me with a note pad taking note on my vitals. All I could hear was a constant beep, beep, beep as if it were my heart monitor. Everything was a complete blur, so with no strength to hold my eyes I fell back out into complete darkness. This time I was in darkness, but my sense of hearing was fully alert. My body was in so much pain that being in the darkness was a place of comfort for me. There was complete silence beside the constant beeping and the nurse occasionally talking. Then after a while, I heard a transporter tell the nurse, "I'm here to take him to his room." She said, "Ok" and unhooked me from a machine; it was at this time I could tell I had tubes running into both my arms and through my nose. As the transporter started moving my bed, the pain in my stomach was unbearable. I could feel every bump as he pushed me, with each one feeling as if I were being stabbed in the gut with a knife. As I was being pushed to the room I was going to, I could tell I had reached my family because I heard my mother's voice say "Oh my God." I peeped into a blur and also saw my older sister Theresa looking at me in disbelief and aww. I closed my eyes back into darkness and they pushed me into a room. Once in my room, I heard the nurses tell my family that I was ok and maybe out for a while and that they would monitor me for any problems. My family agreed and I rested in the darkness I was in. After a while, I could tell my family was getting worried about me because I heard them all saying "He hasn't moved or anything." I could feel my mother's hand gracing my arm, the warmth of her hand was a comfort to my soul, the same as a child at birth first being held by its mother after leaving her womb. As she held my hand praying, I dug deep within in my spirit, gathered all the strength I had in me, and with her hand in mine. I gave her a slight squeeze to let her know I was there and alive. At that moment my mother screamed out, "He just squeezed my hand, he's ok." After I did that, it took everything out of me, so I went back into darkness again. While in my darkness, I could hear the patient in my room next to me. He and his family were all gathered together. He had been shot five times and survived. One-shot was four inches from his heart. When I overheard this, the first thing I thought was, "Damn, I would have been better getting shot, this dude talking and everything." As they continued to talk, he mentioned that whoever shot him didn't get caught and they were still out free. Now with that being said, Prince Georges Hospital has been famous for people coming in there and murdering surviving gunshot victims to keep them from testifying. I heard Theresa say "I'll be right back," and within a few minutes, I was being moved to another room. When we got in the room, I could hear my mother, my girlfriend and everyone saying, "What happened, what's going on?" That's when my sister told them with the guy's shooters still free she wanted me to be safe. Now even in my state of pain, I thought to myself, thank God for my sister being on point. Once visiting hours were over I was there all alone and that's when my walk with God became my strength. All I could think about was Job in the Bible because I had everything going good for me, now this happened, and I couldn't believe it. The next morning a nurse came into my room and told me "Good morning Mr. Ball," she woke me, by this time my eyes were *wide open, I was up, and vibrant. She told me that I had to try to get up, move around because I was at risk of catching pneumonia from sweating in my bed if I just laid there, and if I caught pneumonia I could die. This scared me because dying in the hospital was the last thing I wanted. At this point I thought to myself ok, I got to get up and make it out of here, but as soon as I went to lift up, I was stopped by intense pain in my stomach from the surgery. The pain was so deep that I honestly was scared to look down and see what it looked like. There was a handle that hung over my bed that was for me to lift myself up with, so I struggled and pulled myself up to an upright position. I had to use the bathroom, so I staggered and limped myself into the bathroom. Once I used the bathroom I stood in the mirror and removed my gown to see my stomach. What I saw brought tears to my eyes, there was a bandage that covered my staples in my stomach, but from my stomach around to my back was swollen to the point that I looked deformed. I stared at myself and literally cried. The fact that I was going through this broke my pride. I made it back to sit down in the chair next to my bed. I sat in a deep daydream with a* cold stare, my mind was thinking about what I needed to do in order to get out of there and come back stronger. While the nurse changed my sweaty sheets, emotionally I was at my lowest because I had just sent a new song to Dj Flexx on 95.5. and I was now going to miss my show in New York and Nassau Coliseum. When the nurse finished changing my sheets, she told me that once I got enough strength I would have to try to walk around in order to get stronger, so I could go home. This was the biggest challenge of my life and if I didn't beat it would be my death. That evening my doctor came in and told me that for the first week after my surgery I couldn't eat, so I ate nothing, drank fluids, and worked on getting stronger with getting in and out my bed. It was now Sunday and I knew D.C. Home Jams was coming on that night, so I had my girlfriend call the radio station and tell them of my injuries and illness. That night I had the radio on in my room and when it hit nine o'clock I was all ears on 95.5. When the show came on Dj Flexx said: "We want everyone to keep Marc Shyst in prayer, he's at PG Hospital going through it, we want to lift him up, here is his new song Terror Pitt, and a Trapp on 95.5 WPGC Home Jams." When I heard that my heart smiled as did my mouth, it motivated me to get well and get back to my music. Over the next week, my doctor had me to start eating baby food to help build my digestive system. Along with that, I had to strengthen my lungs to breath normal again. One night in my sleep in the hospital I had a dream, in the dream, a dark-skinned three hundred pound demon dressed in a nightgown skirt, with blond curly hair came in my room. Once she came into my room, she jumped on my neck and started choking me. In the dream, I was losing my breath, but in reality, I was too. I woke out the dream of losing my breath to the point I hit the button for my nurse. When she answered, "Yes, Mr. Ball" I had no wind to respond back, the nurse quickly rushed in, seen me passing out gasping for breath, and put my oxygen mask on my face to resuscitate me. After that event took place, I came to realize that this was more of a spiritual struggle than ever, and my God would heal me. I continued to think of the book of Job, all he went through, and how God restored all back to him. So through it all, I remained praising Gods name and knew I would make it out. It was my third week in recovery, I was feeling stronger and even began walking around the hospital to strengthen myself. I had taken a nap that evening and while I was sleeping I felt someone walk in,when I opened my eyes it was an older man dressed in all black. He greeted at my door as he walked in, he let me know he was Clairece's father, a friend Theresa that I knew. I also knew Clairece's family was in church heavy and her father was a preacher. As he walked in closer to me on my bed he began ministering to me, by the time he was standing near me, my spirit was at ease by his presence. Mr. Higgins stood over me, let me know he had been where I had been, he had seen the days I was facing, and he was there to pray me out of this to go back into the world. With that being said he placed his hands on my forehead and began to pray, while he prayed it was like all was lifted and I knew it was all for a reason. After Mr. Higgings left that day, I continued to rebuild myself over the next few days and was released to go home to get back to my life.

CHAPTER 6

THE STRUGGLE MIXTAPE

(Isaiah 45: 2-3)

2. I will go before you and will level the mountains, I will break down gates of bronze and cut through bars of iron.

3. I will give you hidden treasures, riches stored in secret places, so that you may know that I am the Lord, the God of Israel, who summons you by name.

My first day home from the hospital, I was glad to be out, and on my feet. On my way home I remember looking out of the passenger window in a deep daydream. Life seemed to be more focused to me, the trees, the clouds, everything I laid my eyes on seemed to be clearer, and in living color. When I got home to my apartment I was cool for a few minutes, but about an hour went by and my emotions shifted. I sat down at my kitchen table, had an internal breakdown, all the pain, and humiliation of going through surgery hit me all at once. I had so much anger inside me that I was holding in and it all came out at that moment. With my girlfriend looking at me in wonder,

I fell back in a deep stare while tears began to fill my eyes. I literally cried tears of anger, as my girlfriend watched me fearing what's wrong. I then yelled out while grinding my teeth "I just want to hurt somebody, I want a nigga to feel the same pain I just went through. A nigga better not look at me wrong, say nothing disrespectful or act like he got a problem because I'm a put him in the hurt I was in." As she listened to me she quickly calmed me down and let me know not to think that way. After a while, I cooled down and came back to my senses of rightful thinking. My doctors told me to stay in the house for a month and rest and not to be out and about, but with getting back in the studio on my mind, I knew that wasn't going to happen. I stayed home and rested for two days.   On the second day, I got the keys to my car and headed to the studio. When I called Anton and told him I was home from the hospital, he was excited to hear me on the phone. I told him I was about to head out and come to the studio to see him. He then told me that since I had been gone and in the hospital, the studio had moved. He told me they had moved closer to me in Clinton, Maryland. With excitement still in his voice, he gave me the new address and told me to come through. I left out immediately, as I was headed there I felt a sense of ease because with the studio being in Clinton, Maryland, it only took me about fifteen minutes to get there. When I pulled up, I couldn't wait to see the new studio. I knocked on the door, Anton came, and let me in. The new studio was a lot bigger than before, instead of one room, now we had a lobby area with two studio rooms to work out of. They even had another small room just to make beats. Anton let me know they had all new equipment to make beats, to record now, and that my new stuff would sound even better than before. After touring the new studio and talking with everyone, I started to feel faint. Sofi Green was there; she looked at me and said, "Marc, you look like you lost some weight." Even as she said it, I was getting tired by the minute. I sat around long enough, but quickly realized it took thought, and strength to open and close my eyes. I knew I had been out too long, so I said my goodbyes and left the studio .to head back home. While driving home, I understood why my doctors told me to rest for a month, my body was not fully healed and I needed more time to fully recover. After resting for about two weeks and going back and forth to my doctors, I called the twins and told them I was coming back down to the studio because I was ready to work. When I got there, both Anton and Anthony were working in the beat making room. The beats they were creating had reached another level, they were using all new equipment and it was elevating their sound. While skipping through their new beats I picked one that I liked. I told them "I want to do something to this one." My main focus at that time was to see if my lungs could hold enough wind to push out a full song. I wrote to the song that day in the studio and hit the booth that night. The song came out good, so with no real focus on what to do with the song, we decided to keep recording and building more songs.

With City Vibe moving to a bigger location, it brought in bigger names and industry artist. One of the groups that came through frequently was Prophet Jones, they had a big record deal a few years prior and were rebuilding their career with production from the twins. I used to tell the twins all the time, "Man I want to do a song with them," and the twins would say, "We got you homie." Prophet Jones would come through on the regular to record and I began to build my own relationship with them to the point we became cool. So after a few months went by they needed a rapper on one of their songs and my hopes became a reality. The twins asked me to write a rap to their song and I delivered a smash verse. Afterward, I was hype because at this point, this was the first song I had done with an industry artist. With my song with Prophet Jones in my catalog, I had built up a few new songs with my producers. A lot of rappers that the twins produced for were really picky and lacked self-confidence. They all wanted beats that would make them sound better than what they were. They would say to Anton and Anthony, make me a hit twin. I used to watch as a lot of local rappers would go through all the beats that they played for them and they wouldn't find a beat they were looking for. This left a lot of unused beats, beats I would take and write smashes to. Now at this time, I had about thirty songs I had put together. We were ready to sit down and put together an album for me. So we had a meeting, me, the twins and pops along with the people who worked at City Vibe. We all decided to put together my project, push it locally to start my buzz in the streets, and shop it around for a record deal. So over the next few days, I picked out the songs I liked and the ones that would make the album. All of my songs had a different edge, so it was hard at first to put together, but with careful observation, I came up with about eighteen songs of my best work. After we picked and agreed to the songs that were going on the album, we had to come up with a name. I had the idea of calling it "The Struggle," because of all that I had been through to get to this point. When I put the idea on the table everyone thought it was a good name. While putting the name together, I thought it would be a good idea to call it a mixtape because the songs on it were all versatile and gave a variety of sound. So it was final, we would call the project, "The Struggle Mixtape Volume 1." During the time I was working on releasing my project the state of hip hop was in an all-out war. The Tupac and Biggie beef were now revitalized by the G Unit and Murder Inc. beef. I myself kept my composure from all the riff-raff and remained true to my art of creating within my reality. I never changed my direction of creativity knowing that my origin and persona would surface to light one day. So with my new project under wraps, we all thought that what was needed at the time was a visual, an official video. The twins had a relationship with an up and coming videographer from Maryland name Chris "Broadway" Romero. Broadway had a company called Capital Gainz, he had an artist he managed and worked with named Bliss. Broadway would bring Bliss through to City Vibe to record and that's how I became acquainted with both of them. At the time of me needing a video done, Broadway had produced the last video of the late Big Pun, which was an animated video. Being that Big Pun had passed away that video made his portfolio stronger. Broadway was the only industry video man in D.C. at the time who was on top of his game. The twins worked out an agreement with Broadway, we picked a song of mine called Kaypaz and we set a date to start production of my first video. Broadway had done animation videos before, but this was his first live shoot, and I was honored he was going to be the first director I would be working with. I myself actually loved the process of creating a video because Broadway actually let me shoot ideas to him on visuals for the song. As I gave them to him, he added his expertise to create a script that we could put together and make a video. So with everything in place we all picked a date to start and in two days, we nailed it. The video Kaypaz was shot and recorded and the only thing left to do was editing. Now the editing was a part of making a video that I never knew about and wanted to learn. So Broadway would let me come over his house to see the process sometimes and just let me kick it. I remember the first time at his house, I sat down where he worked, and on his computer was an animation project for G Unit. I mean it looked amazing what he was doing, he had the G Unit logo doing things that only he could imagine. I asked him in excitement, "You doing work for G Unit," and he just smiled and with a nonchalant attitude said, "Yea a little something I'm putting together for them." When I saw that I knew he would blow up one day soon. After a month or so of work, it was finally done and Broadway killed it. I was so happy when he showed me the finished project. I couldn't do anything, but smile like it was Christmas and I was five years old. I took the video over to City Vibe and we all knew it was time to move on to get this album out.

We knew at that time that I had the best music in D.C. because every relevant rapper in D.C. was coming to *our studio to record. With that in mind we wanted to have the best looking CD that D.C. had yet to be seen, so with Broadway in our corner, we went back to him to help me design an album cover that would raise the bar of an underground album, and he did just that. I did a photoshoot, and he took the pictures and made them come to life. When it was all done, we decided to go through Disc Makers to print the album because with Disc Makers we would have the professional look that we wanted to kill the streets of D.C., Maryland, and Virginia. The twins made a few calls to the Disc Makers office in New York, got the templates we needed, and had Broadway put it all in proper places to be printed and it was done. Instead of just sending everything to the office and negotiating on the phone, we all drove up to New York to the Disc Makers office and put it all together. We stayed overnight after the meeting and came back home the next morning. When we got back from New York, we had two weeks before the CD's would be back, so I knew I had two weeks to get ready to set up a plan to push them out. Putting a plan together for me was easy, with me having the hottest music out and now the best-looking package, the plan was* simple. Put my CD in every store that would sell it and make sure everyone knew it was there. With two weeks seeming like two years, I got the call from Anthony telling me the CD's had been delivered today and they were at the studio. As soon as I heard that I shot down there like superman with a distress call. As I broke down the door to get in, I could see the boxes on the floor, Anthony looked at me nodding his head and with a smile on his face he said: "They look good man." He gave me a copy and I was astonished, I just stared at it until seemingly I fell into the CD. It had everything that an industry album had, it was wrapped in plastic and labeled as an official release, and I was so happy and ready that I took a box of one hundred, grabbed eighty posters and got to work. When I left with those one hundred CD's I did just as I had planned to do. In a week's time, I had done consignment deals with all the major record stores in D.C. that would carry my CD. I had hit every mixtape spot and all the mom and pop stores from Maryland to Virginia. In all, I had about twenty stores on deck with it and had pushed the word out to the streets that it was available for sale. With my new CD moving in the stores, I spent a lot of time out promoting

rather than being in the studio. One day while out
promoting, Anton called me and said: "Shyst hurry up and
get to the studio, some dudes from G Unit down here."
When he said that my heart jumped and I headed down in
the direction of the studio. While driving there, my mind
was all over the place thinking, how, why, and what would
make G Unit be in D.C., and at our studio? As I was getting
closer, my mind recalled a story I read about 50 cent's
former partner and associate Bang Em Smurf leaving G
Unit over a fall out he and 50 cent had. I don't know why
that popped up in my head, but as soon as I got to the
studio and went in the recording room, there he was, Bang
Em Smurf with about six goons with him. When I came in
they were listening to beats by the twins. Anton
introduced me to them and we locked in with light
conversation as I observed them and they observed me.
The six dudes with Bang Em were all street niggas and they
had the look of wolves in their eyes. Not as if they were
scared, but as if when things went wrong they were ready
to pop off. Bang Em then played the G Unit diss song in
the studio as he explained to me his new movement, Silver
Back Gorillaz and that he wasn't fucking with 50 anymore.

We talked for a while as they set up to come back the next time they were in town and Bang Em introduced me to his new artist Domination. Domination was cool and it was all good vibes while they were there, when they were leaving there hard looks became slight smiles and they were more relaxed. While we were saying our peace and goodbyes, I gave Bange Em and his crew all copies of my new CD. As I gave it to Bang Em he looked at it and said "Marc Shyst, that's what's up," so Bang Em and I switched numbers to keep in touch and they departed the studio after their short stay. With everyone that heard me saying my voice sounded like 50 cent, I now had just put my music in the hands of his right-hand man, his ex-general and I was curious to hear how he thought I sounded. So after about three days I reached out and called Bang Em to touch base with him and see how he was. When I called him, he picked up the phone on blast, hype as if he was in the studio recording. "Shyst Waddup, Ay yo we fucking with that CD." When he said that it was a healing answer to my curiosity. We spoke for a minute and he mentioned that he loved one of the songs on my project called "What the Deal Is." Bang Em was hype about it and wanted to know if his artist Domination could do a remix on it with me. For me, this was an honor for him to even ask to collaborate with me. I told him, "No problem bro, it's done." He let me know that they would be coming back down to D.C. in a few weeks and we would hook up then.

In the meantime, I was moving in the streets a hundred miles and running. With my new CD out, I had moved on from selling my clothes to moving drugs in the street. I still sold my clothing line, but at this point, my new connections had me on another level. I had my hands on it all, from cocaine to hydro and with my new CD on every shelf, I was growing fast in the streets of D.C., Maryland, and Virginia. Now with meeting up with Bang Em Smurf, I had New York in my sights. Two weeks went by and Bang Em hit me up to let me know they were coming back in town for a show in Maryland in a couple of days. So the night of their show, I met them there at the club right outside D.C. called The Spot. When I got there Bang Em and his entourage were outside about thirty deep. They were arguing and angered with the promoter because they did no promotion and the crowd was weak. After going back and forth with the club, Bang Em was like,

"Fuck it, let's hit the studio with my nigga Marc Shyst." I
had my little cousin Carol with me who was a gutter little
dude and a real live shooter. I was armed with two forty-
five caliber pistols, so I could protect Bang Em and his crew
if needed. So we left the club and dropped his entourage
off at their hotel. When we dropped them off Bang Em
and his man Bolo got in my car and they followed with a
car behind us. At the moment they were in my back seat,
the rap game became real-life reality, these were two real
goons I had seen on 50 cents Get Rich or Die Trying DVD
sitting in my back seat and I had every intention to protect
them with my life as we headed to the studio. While
driving to the studio I asked Bang Em about how they
pushed their records in the streets, being as though he had
helped launch 50 cents career with mixtapes in New York.
He gave me a few pointers to do and then he unloaded the
real science on me about how to take the game as they did
with G Unit. As he talked I soaked it all in like a sponge,
and I could tell he believed in me to even give me what he
did. When we got to the studio it had to be about twelve
in the morning. We settled in and I made a few calls to
have a couple of girls I knew come through and keep his

crew company, and with me hustling, I had all the blueberry dro they could blow. We played a few beats and Domination, Bang Em, and I laid three songs down in the studio until about four in the morning. What came out was really aggressive street hits. While recording his crew let me know they were banging my CD in New York and it gave me encouragement. Bang Em also let me know he would do anything that he could to help me and I could tell he was sincere about it, which was the very thing I respected about Bang Em. That night he never said anything bad about 50 cent, he just focused on us recording solid music. When we were done I took them back to their hotel and everything was cool. When they got out of my car and I got home that night, I knew I was in the right place with the right people. The next evening I called Bang Em to make sure they made it back to New York ok. He let me know they did and told me to come up to New York to southside queens, I told him I would and that the songs we did I would send them that week after they were mixed and mastered. Bang Em was excited about them and let me know he was going to put one of the songs on their new mixtape they were dropping in New

York. This was major for me because it was taking me from a local artist to a serious national one, one that was doing what no other rapper in D.C. was doing at that time. My relationship with Bang Em was a prosperous and life evolving one. During the time of us talking back and forth, they released a series of mixtapes that I was on that eventually landed them a record deal. A deal I was proud to say I saw him work hard to attain.

As I continued in the streets with promoting my CD, my confidence was on another level, we had all the connections and plugs with the people in D.C. we needed, but we wanted to reach the world. So one day while at the studio putting some things together Anton was like, "Let's take the CD's and drive out to Cali and hit the studio out there." I had never been to California, so I was like "Yeah, let's do it." So we grabbed about five hundred CD's loaded up in the City Vibe promo van and left the east coast on a road trip to California. Before we left I called Bang Em and asked him if he knew anyone out in California he could plug me with because I was about to head out there. His response was "You about to be in Cali? We'll be out there the end of this week!!!! Yeah Yeah Yeah." So it was a wrap *and I knew he would help me be in the right places and I couldn't believe he and his crew were going to be out there, but that's how God's plan works out when it's his destiny. When the twins and I left out from the studio in Clinton to head to Cali, they told me it would be a two-day drive. With that being said I packed all I needed, I had the twins make a CD of beats for me to write to, my earphones, my pad and pen and about a quarter pound of weed smoke on. I asked the twins if they mind me bringing my pistol just in case, they were like "Nah bring it." So I did, along with my bag of clothes and we headed out. From the time we pulled out until we made our first stop in North Carolina I had my earphones on and writing new songs. I would have helped drive if they needed, but since they knew the direction, they let me lay back and write songs. I also brought my camcorder with us too, so I could document the whole trip. Every time we stopped I pulled out my camera, every state we traveled through, I pulled out my camera. For me, this trip brought me closer to God and the earth he created because in every state we hit you could see how it was unique in its own way. From the landscapes to the temperatures and even the different* accents in voices of the people and I loved it. After fifty-two hours of being on the road, we finally were pulling into the hills and mountains of California. Before we came to California Anton and Anthony would always tell me that once I went out there that I would never be the same and now that I was there I understood what they were saying. Our plan once out there was to hit the studio and record a song called "Push It" that I had done a rough draft to back at City Vibe. So the twins knew a lady in California named Samone that worked at Paramount Recording Studios, one of the major studios near Hollywood. The first day or so the twins took me around for a little sightseeing as they visited old friends they had known. While riding through the streets of California, I could feel that essence that my brother Tupac was talking about in his rhymes. Everywhere we went I would kick it with real dudes from out there and slowly but surely they would put me on a game about Cali. Things like what hood I was in, what gangs were around, and what colors you could wear and why. Things that don't matter on the east coast, but in California, it could cost you your life. We moved around for a few days, ate at all the famous California spots and then it was time for business. So Anthony called up Samone to see if she could get us in Paramount for a session. When he called her I could tell he was kind of hesitant and I didn't know why at first, but when he got off the phone with her I found out. When he hung up, he sighed and told me and Anton, "Ok, we in there, we just got to go out to her house and see her tomorrow to set it up." When he said that Anton kind of laughed and shook his head, as he did I asked in curiosity, "What's wrong, why y'all laughing?" That's when Anton said "Because that's Anthony old crush," and then laughed again. This meant that if we were going to get the studio time, Anthony would have to take one for the team. Being outside D.C. and in California had opened my creative perspective to another level. The whole time there all I could think about was "This is what Tupac was talking about in his songs." It literally felt like he was my tour guide that prepped me for a trip, and he was right there with me. The next day we did as planned and went to Samone's house that was right outside of Hollywood. When we got to her house, we pulled in on a street right in front of a storefront. Where we parked at didn't look like anyone's house, but then we got out and walked through an alley that leads to Samone's apartment. When we got to her door I was curious about how this woman looked since Anthony was acting skeptical about going over there. Anthony knocked and Samone came to the door and opened it, as we walked in they all greeted and then Anton and Anthony said: "Samone this is Marc the rapper we told you about." As I took a look at her, she was kind of cool as my first thought, she greeted me with a warm smile and we shook hands. Samone was a white woman, but down to earth, she had a sort of seventies hippie style and vibe to her and that was the mood of her place. As I sat down I thought to myself, "I know she got to smoke weed." And sure enough after about twenty minutes of being there, she pulled out a bong and hit it. So Samone and Anthony had to go to the studio to set things up for us to go in and record the next day. As they were leaving Samone told Anton "You guys can just chill here while we're gone this won't take, but a few hours or so." Anton agreed, so they took the van and left me and Anton at Samone's. By the time they returned, it had been about four hours that went by and seemed like we were there all day. Anton and I were ready to go and get out

- 121 -

and about. Anthony came in and told us everything was good and we were scheduled to go in the studio tonight at eight o'clock. With the time being around four-thirty pm, we only had a few hours to run around before we hit the studio. So we left out to get something to eat, and by the time we were done it was time to hit the studio and I was ready. As we were heading there I felt like I was going to the main event show and I was the premiere act. When we got to Paramount, from the outside it looked just like a regular warehouse type of building with a bar gated door entrance, but once they buzzed us in the studio it was a state of the art facility. In the studio, they had three major recording rooms, Studio A, Studio B, and Studio C. Studio C was the biggest studio and that's where all the major stars recorded, so that's where we chose to record. While setting up to record, Samone let us know that Tupac, Biggie, Master P and Brandi along with other industry artist had recorded in the same room. This made me feel empowered by the fact that I was now there and about to record. It made me feel as though one day I would be on that level and would have the stature of those artists that were there. As we prepared, our engineer came in to record the session. Anton and Anthony recorded me at City Vibe, but this was a whole new ball game. I was recording on an SSL board, which is the Mercedes Benz of recording boards. A piece of equipment that was worth over a half of million dollars. The engineer was a small weird white guy with spikey red hair. He came in and introduced his self as Guy. The guy was very professional while I recorded and I could tell he knew what he was doing. As I recorded he knew how to put me in perfect placement and when to let me be me. I executed with perfection and Guy helped me to do it. When I was finished recording I came out of the booth and went back into the mixing room with Guy and the twins and that's when it all came out. Anton said, "Marc guess who Guy used to work with?" I was like who, and Anton told me "Tupac." Right when he said that my heart skipped a beat. So Guy looked at me and said: "Yea I was the one who played the guitar on Tupac's song, me and my girlfriend." At this point, I was stuck on Guy like a student with his professor. I had question after question. He told us he worked for Death Row as an engineer for a while until he left there and did some other things while he wrapped up *with recording my song, I just walked around the studio in awe at the fact that someone who worked with Tupac actually worked with me. It was so overwhelming that I had to take it all in without going crazy. Guy put his finishing touch on my record, we all said our peace and goodbyes and we left the studio that night with a new hit record and I had the experience of my life with an engineer who worked with my spiritual predecessor and favorite artist Tupac.*

With our new song recorded and running around California, it was about time for us to head back home to the east coast. Up to this point I hadn't talked to or heard from Bang Em yet, so I reached out to him to see what's up. When he picked up, he told me he would be landing in Las Vegas tomorrow, and to come holler at him. So we stayed another night in California and with New Year's Eve 2004 tomorrow we knew we were in for a wild night in Vegas. The next morning Bang Em called me when they landed and we headed out to Vegas. With Vegas being a few hours away it was almost nightfall as we pulled in. As we got near Las Vegas I called Bang Em again to see where he was at. He let me know he was at a studio, but he didn't know the directions. During this time there weren't

smartphones with GPS, so we went off of old school

directions. So as we talked he put me on hold and he put a

dude on the phone that leads me there from where I was

at. The guy on the phone I later found out was C-Bo, a

legendary rapper on the west coast. When we got to the

studio, it was packed with people inside, and an entourage

of real soldiers. As Bang Em introduced me to everyone

they all received me with love like I was one of their own.

He took me over to a dude and was like "Shyst this my man

C-Bo, Bo this my nigga Shyst from D.C." C-Bo looked at me

with a smile, greeted me and said: "What up young

nigga?" I spoke back to him, but at the time I honestly still

didn't know exactly who he was. As I observed everyone in

the studio, I recognized the rapper Spice 1 in the corner

chilling. Spice 1 was a legend in D.C., from his west coast

gangster songs, and the smash hit from the movie Menace

to Society. I kept my chill as we fired up the best west

coast green I had chocked on and everyone kicked it.

Outside the studio was nothing but big trucks, Benzes, and

expensive cars, a real boss type of atmosphere. When

Spice 1 walked by me at one point, I introduced myself and let him know I was a fan of his music and it was a pleasure meeting him. He was intrigued by me being from D.C. and out there in the mix. We didn't talk for too long while everyone did their thing. As I observed C-Bo in the studio though, I could tell he was a sure enough boss, he had a Suge Knight demeanor, but was a humble dude with it. He was back and forth on his phone, in and out of the studio and making sure we were all ok. With it being New Year's Eve, and coming up on eleven o'clock pm, C-Bo was like "Come on y'all, let's hit the strip and get into something." When we left the studio we were like fifteen to twenty cars deep. C-Bo leads us all to the Las Vegas strip, where we pulled into a lot and parked. Once in the parking lot we all gathered with doors open, music bumping in every direction like the party was right there, but that wasn't the half of it. We stopped at the casino after casino, one after another while casino hopping we bumped into Fredro Star outside of a club we were going in. As we walked to the club doors, it was about eleven forty-five and we were trying to get into a celebrity party for the New Year. As Fredro walked by me, I said what's up to him and he looked at me and said: "What's up D.C. right?" I cracked a *smile and laughed at the fact he remembered me. With about thirty people with us now, we managed to get into the party. With us in street clothes and with nothing, but gangsters with us, when we got in the club I couldn't believe the A list of stars that were there. As we stood on the floor I saw Joe Jackson, Jermaine Jackson, and the entire Jackson family, excluding Michael and Janet. I saw a lot of actors and celebrities around me that just walked by me like it was nothing and I was supposed to be there. At that moment I could tell that C-Bo was a real live legend and powerful man because all this was nothing to him. When twelve o'clock hit, we all toasted to the New Year and was out the door and off to another club. This time we all jumped on a party bus and road to another casino with a club. A lot of clubs refused us because of our attire, but C-Bo kept us moving on to the next spot. After it had hit about three o'clock we all headed back to our cars. Bang Em told me, "Shyst you can chill with us tonight bra." So the twins and I all followed C-Bo and Bang Ems cars back to a house in Vegas. As we followed them we pulled into a complex of upper-class houses. We then pulled outside of C-Bo's house, a beautifully built mini-mansion. With me* and the twins and Bang Em's entourage, we were about fifteen people deep, not to mention C-Bo's right-hand man 151. As we all found a spot on the living room floor to sleep, me and Bang Em stayed awake in conversation. As we talked Bang Em was throwing questions at me to see what kind of business I was doing in the street. He then told me to come upstairs where we went into C-Bo's master bedroom with 151 and that's where the fellowship happened at about five o'clock in the morning. As we chopped it up blowing weed, C-Bo broke the game down on how the streets of the west coast ran the game. He took us into a world only a true boss could project for us. He let us know of all the NBA, and NFL players that got robbed out there and how the gangs ran the industry. I was in awe of the stories of rappers in the industry that would come out to the west coast and call on him for protection. Periodically C-Bo would ask Bang Em if he heard of certain rappers that were from New York to check their credibility, it was then that I understood the rap game was bigger than a game, it was real. As the morning came we all crashed out, I went back downstairs and laid out on the floor and rested myself. I woke early the next morning to the sun shining and beautiful Las, Vegas weather. As soon as I woke up, I looked up and Bang Em was already a step ahead of me woke. We start smoking again early in the morning as we talked more and then we ran out of blunts to roll and that's when Bang Em tested my heart. Bang Em was like "Hey yo Shyst go upstairs and ask Bo if he got any blunts," I looked at him thinking, this nigga want me to go up there and wake this man up for some blunts, but ok I'm a show him my heart. As I went to C-Bo's room and knocked on the door he didn't answer, so I called out to him "Bo...Hey yo Bo," I opened the door and he was knocked out sleep with 151 layings on guard beside him, that's how serious these dudes were, real gangster shit. C-Bo woke out his sleep and I asked him for the blunts and he looked at me like "This nigga woke me up," but then he said, "All right I got you" and I closed his door and went back downstairs. Two minutes later C-Bo came to the top of the stairs and looked at me with a serious, but humorous look and threw down a box of blunts to me. I could tell he was thinking in his head, "This little nigga don't get no sense." As we smoked and talked more that's when Bang Em told me who Bo was with Tupac and his *history. I knew we had a two-day trip ahead of us, so I kicked it for a little while longer and then told everyone we were heading back east. Before I left, I went out to the van and grabbed a couple of my CD's and came back in and gave them to C-Bo. We all said our peace and the twins and I pulled out and left Las Vegas and headed straight back to Washington, D.C.*

CHAPTER 7

VISION COMING TRUE

(NUMBERS 12:6)

He said, hear now my words if there is a prophet among you, I the Lord shall make myself known to him in a dream.

When we left Las Vegas headed back to D.C., the twins decided to take an alternate route home. When we drove across to California, we came through Texas and New Mexico. Going back home they took the northern route, which took us through Colorado and a lot of unexpected winter weather. Leaving out of Vegas was smooth sailing, I still had my earphones on and writing to my beat CD. I had managed to write about ten new songs and counting. As I had done before on our trip to Cali I would occasionally doze off in the van as the twins drove. Coming back was no different, I fell asleep about two hours into the trip and then I was awakened by Anton and Anthony arguing over how to drive. When I opened my eyes it was if we were driving in clouds of falling feathers, except the clouds of feathers was a real live snowstorm.

Driving through the snow was nothing new to me and at that time I didn't think anything of it, so I fell back to sleep thinking it was just something slight. The next time I woke up was to a loud...Bang...Boom. It startled me because it was loud like a shotgun let off. When I jumped out of my sleep to see what it was we were crashed against a hill of rocks on an off-ramp. Anthony had lost control in the snow trying to pull over at a gas station to get off the road to allow time for the snow to clear up. When he crashed Anton looked at him and yelled "What you doing Anthony" and with a surprised look, Anthony hollered back, "The van slid, I couldn't hold it." After we crashed, Anthony pressed on the gas and it was clear we were stuck because the van just revved up and the tires spun as he kept hitting the gas. At that point, I got slightly worried that we would be stuck on this pullover the ramp, but with him continually spinning the tires we slid off the rocks and caught grip enough to continue moving. We pulled into the gas station in Colorado and filled up with gas, that's when Anton got behind the wheel and started driving to give Anthony an opportunity to rest. When Anton got back on the highway it seemed like the snow had begun falling harder. The snowflakes were the size of golf balls and they were coming down at a fast pace. I was up at this point and at full attention as we drove on the highway. As Anton was driving it seemed as though we were the only car in sight, the only vehicles moving through the snowstorm were tractor-trailers. Besides the weather conditions at that time, the other dangers on the road were that we were high in the mountains where there were a lot of cliffs that in the current conditions could be dangerous. When we were in darkness on the highway we were at our greatest risk because if we were to get stuck in the snow again there was no way anyone would be able to come and save us in this terrible snowstorm, and if they did, by the time they got there we would have been buried in snow and possibly frozen to death. So while Anton was driving I was sitting up so far in my seat in the back, I was damn near in between him and Anthony in the front seat. Every time a tractor-trailer would come through, I would tell Aton to stay close behind the tractor-trailer, so we could follow him through the snow. But every time he got behind one, he would let the tractor get ahead too far and eventually he would lose the trail of the tractor-trailer. After he managed to lose the trail of about five tractor-trailers from driving too slow, Anton decided to pull over at the next rest stop to hopefully let the snow die down. When we got to the rest stop there was no slowing down of the snowfall, so I suggested to let me drive to get us out of the snowstorm. With nothing else to lose, Anton agreed to let me drive. When I got behind the wheel of the van, this was my first time being behind the wheel the entire trip. Although I was driving, it wasn't to be able to sightsee, it was in a desperate attempt to save our lives and prayerfully get us to safety. When I got behind the wheel I knew I was the only thing that would keep us alive, so I strapped on my seat belt and pulled out the rest stop onto the highway. Once I got on the highway the snow was so thick on the ground the van barely caught traction in order for me to maneuver the vehicle successfully. I waited patiently for a tractor-trailer to come to pass, so I could ride his trail out of the snow. About ten minutes went by and I could see a tractor-trailer approaching in the rearview mirror, and as soon as he passed me in the fast lane I jumped behind it like I was chained to its bumper. I was driving at the speed of about sixty-five miles per hour before the tractor-trailer passed, but now that I was following his trail I had picked up to speeds of eighty miles per hour in the snow to keep up with him. With doing eighty miles per hour in the van, the van was shaking like it was about to fall apart. While driving behind the tractor-trailer the only thing on my mind was if I lose his trail, we were going to die in Colorado, and my train of thought was that if I speed through the storm, we could beat it and get to clear skies and safety. As I was driving at top speed, Anton and Anthony's faces were focused on the road, and it was as quiet as nap time in the van. I mean you could have heard a needle drop in there. One of the dangers of driving in the mountains of Colorado was that on the highways there were no guard rails, just straight cliffs that fell down off the side of the mountains, so if you slid off, you more than likely did so to your death. Along with keeping up with this tractor-trailer, I was focused on staying on the highway and not swerving off the side of a cliff. With the fear of dying in my head, it seemed like we were driving in a never-ending storm. Every second felt like a minute and every minute felt like an hour, but after trailing behind the tractor-trailer at top speeds of eighty-five miles an hour in the snow for about an hour, my plan worked. We got through the snowfall to clear skies, and we all had a sigh of relief. When I knew we were good and far out of the snow, I went to pull over and let the twins take back over driving. As I was approaching a stop sign that gave you the option of taking a right or left I hit the brakes, but the van kept sliding forward. While the van was sliding I was praying it would stop before crossing the stop sign, but it didn't. As the van crossed through the stop sign, what was approaching was a deep cliff, and when the van kept sliding to the edge of the cliff, I looked over at Anthony and as the van tipped to fall over the cliff we all hollered "AAAHHHHHH," as if we were about to fall in an endless pit. The endless pit was a hill of grass that we slid down into a bank. After smashing into the grassy bank, miraculously I just hit the gas and proceeded to drive back on the ramp to pull over at the gas station. While pulling over we all had the same thought, that an angel just saved our lives again. When I got in the back seat I felt at ease, so much at ease that when Anton took back over driving I was worn out from the driving and fell back to sleep. The next time I woke up, we were in sunny skies, it seemed like it took forever to get back home, but within the next four hours or so we were back home in D.C. After being on the road for about two weeks it felt good to be back home with my family. The day I got home I made up my mind that I would take a break from the studio for a few days to rest before I went back in, but my trip to California wasn't through with me. When I sat my bags down and got myself together, I was home for about two hours when my cell phone rang. As I looked at the name on it, it said Bang Em Smurf, my first thought was I wonder what bra want, so in excitement, I picked up like "Whaddup bra?" He replied back to me "Shyst, I got somebody who wants to talk to you." So he handed the phone off and the next voice I hear was C-Bo. When he got on the phone, I could tell he was smoking because he was inhaling and talking. He asked me "Whaddup little bra, why you didn't tell me you get down like that?" I told him in a nonchalant way "You know, I do a little something." He told me that he wanted me to come back out there to put some music down and let's drop something. I agreed and told him "Let's do it." He then said, "I'm a fly you out in a few weeks and get it in." I told him I would get his number from Bang Em and we went get it done. Then

Bang Em got back on the phone and I told him "Appreciate that bra," he replied to me "It ain't nothing bra, let's get it," and we got off the phone. When I hung up, I couldn't believe it, I felt like my brother Tupac had really reached out to me through C-Bo and now I was about to live out my dream. I had thoughts of making it big one day and it all happened as I could never imagine. See, once I found out that C-Bo recorded with Tupac and really knew him, it was as if Tupac made a way for me to blow. C-Bo was one of the biggest underground artists in California and was well respected by all the industry artists in the game. He had sold millions of records as an independent artist and he knew the formula for success. After it all sunk in I immediately called Anton and told him the news. I was excited for them as well because if I was in California doing music with C-Bo, I could get their production heard by the industry. So when I told them what C-Bo wanted to do, they were ready to get back in the studio as soon as possible to put another album together. That day I pulled out my Tupac CD, "All Eyes On Me," and played trading war stories all day, that was the song C-Bo had recorded with Tupac, and the song Tupac labeled C-Bo a bald head nut. When "All Eyes On Me" was released, rapping was the furthest thing from my mind, and now after all I had been through, I felt that the voice I heard from God and the path I had taken to get here was all for a greater cause than I knew at the time. I shared the news with my family, but kept it to me and my producers for the sake of there was a lot of work still needed to be done. I stayed at home for two days to recuperate from traveling and to spend time with my family and then I rushed back to the studio to put a plan together again with the twins and City Vibe. Once I got back to the studio, the twins and I sat down to decide what we wanted to do. At this point, we had sold over three thousand CDs of "The Struggle Mixtape," and counting. There were people that were even bootlegging it and it was everywhere in the streets. With the awareness out, I just wanted to put together an official album that was not a mixtape of assorted songs, but an album from my heart. We agreed to get it done, and I dropped the title to them and called it "Vision Coming True." The title was a statement of faith that the vision God had given me about my music and my prophecy to hip hop was now coming true. As soon as we all agreed to the project we got *straight to work. Now with all the other projects from my demo to The Struggle Mixtape, Anton and Anthony would already have beats that were made and I would select from them. With this album we wanted to do something different, we wanted to do all-new production from scratch with me right there in the studio. So before we started I went back home grabbed a few clothes and materials and came back that night to get started. Once I got back, I had everything I needed to get started. The twins immediately began to make beats, they were in both studios at the same time and it sounded so surreal. Surreal because as an artist this was the attention I always wanted and now it was real and actually in my forefront. Most of the first beats they created were party and club beats, which was an easy task for me. The first songs I recorded came out good, and now we wanted an album cut. So with our connection with the group Prophet Jones, we wanted to get them on a feature. That's when Anthony started playing around with a few samples and came up with an old school beat from Teddy Pendergrass called "My Place." After the beat was done and complete the twins had our man Hollywood from Prophet Jones stop by the next day* and lay the hook on the song, which was a rendition of Teddy Pendergrass's vocals. When it was all said and done, Hollywood delivered the hook on point, the only thing that was left for me to do was to drop my vocals on it and take the song to the next level. With the hook on the beat now, I had Anthony play the song back over a few times in the studio with the volume on high. This song was something different and my challenge was to create a hit that reached the world and that's what I did. After listening to the beat for about forty-five minutes I had come up with two verses of a smash hit. When I was done I told Anthony, "I'm done bra let's lay this joint." I went in and dropped my vocals and it was done. When they played the song back, everyone in the studio gathered in the room with heads nodding and moving to the groove of the beat. I had recorded a lot of songs at this point, but with this song being an old school classic it drew in an audience of listeners that I never reached before. With a classic hit now on the album with an industry feature, it was time to make something different that was out of thought for anything local. So Anton went in the beat making room and came up with a beat that was dark and

epic, not an average hip hop song to dance to, but a song
that you could tell a story to. When Anton finished the
beat, he arranged it and did some fine-tuning to it, and
after about thirty minutes he was done. I then went in my
creative mode and let my imagination take me to a place
where the instruments of the beat he had made were the
soundtrack to my life. With me not so long ago
overcoming a near-death experience with surgery, I came
up with a song called "Scar." Scar was a detailed song that
gave insight into the process of my surgery. Not only was
it about me going through surgery, but it also depicted my
life and the life of Job in the Holy Bible. When I finished
writing the song it had taken me to an emotional level of
writing, something I had never done, and when I went in
the booth to record it, it was like healing myself with my
testimony. When the song was done and the small group
of artists and people who were at the studio daily heard it,
it captured them. I can remember one artist named A
Hundred Kay, we called him Kal. Kal heard the song and
because he had been shot and survived, it was his favorite
song. Every time he would come by the studio he would
holler out "Man I'm trying to hear that scar joint." It was a

compliment to me since he was also an artist, and my song motivated him. By this time we were about eight songs in and I hadn't left the studio in a week. I had been there around the clock every day working on my album and the work ethic was paying off. Even though I never left the studio, the studio was our sort of playhouse, so I just had everything come to me. At times there would be endless amounts of girls, we had all the smoke we wanted and we created a fun atmosphere there. An atmosphere to me that was my home and a place where I could release my creativity. With the process of this album coming along, I stayed in the studio for another week until we were done and wrapped it up. Once we were done we all knew that I had put together a hit album, and the next process was to get it mixed and mastered. So we got an engineer by the name of Teddy Davis to come in, put his touches on my album and it went through the roof. The album "Vision Coming True," was everything I hoped it would be. I took my spiritual side and my testimonies from the street and created a timeless underground classic. I had dropped so many smash hits on this album that everyone who would hear it, automatically knew that it would eventually get me a record deal. Me on the other hand, once I was finished, I reached back out to C-Bo to follow up on his offer and to check on him, since it had been a few weeks that passed and I hadn't received a call from him. When I called, his manager at the time notified me that he had been locked up and was in jail. When I heard that, it kind of killed the hopes I had, but I knew after he had been released that the type of person he was, we would still hook up. With C-Bo being locked up I still had to stay focused on the mission at hand and worked on getting this album to the next level. After everything was said and done with my album, the reality was that Manistyles were producers and City Vibe was a recording studio. That was the tools it took to get the album done, but to get the album to the next level would take management and a record label. So while the twins and all the new investors reached out to everyone they could to get me a deal with my new album, we decided to hold out on releasing it until we found the right avenue that would land me a major record deal.

CHAPTER 8

THE POP OFF 1

(1 TIMOTHY 6:12)

Fight the good fight of the faith. Take hold of the eternal life to which you were called when you made your good confession in the presence of many witnesses.

After finishing recording the Vision Coming True album we all continued on pushing the project and pursuing to ultimately obtain a record deal with it. Although we had a hit smash album, we held off releasing it as we anticipated getting a record deal. Even with this good news, there was still a void and it left me with a missing piece of the puzzle. We had the Struggle Mixtape project in several mom and pop stores and it was getting the awareness from everyone that it touched, but I felt like it wasn't getting to the core of the people in the streets that I was in touch with. I was getting support, but people would buy my CD and tell me it cranked and that it was tight and such and such, then go into conversation like, "You hear that new 50 cents or you hear that new Ja Rule."

I would just continue talking and converse, but I knew I had to go stronger for the streets to reach them. So I went in deep, thought of what to do and how to create a project that would make my followers and anyone who knew me stop and wonder who this is and make them respect my creative craft. Along with bringing my street element, I wanted to do something to make the record industry see that D.C. was not only a city of Go-Go bands, but that hip hop and rap were on the come up and I was the rapper to bring it to the forefront. What I came up with was called The Pop Off. The Pop Off was a strategic shot fired that would make everyone aware someone was shooting and to pay attention to where the shots were coming from. The Pop off represented a revolutionary movement in hip hop and the start of the strategic war. In theory, The Pop Off would bring respect and substance for D.C. rappers. Not only was being aware of the shots important, but who was doing the shooting, in this case, a rapper named Marc Shyst. So I gathered all the tracks that I had wrote in the van going and coming from California and stayed in the studio recording. The first song to set it off was a song called, However Whenever Whatever, which ended up

being a nonstop aggressive track with no hook, just
straight flow. That song would set the tone and energy for
the rest of the mixtape. The Pop Off was a total one
hundred and eighty-degree change from the Struggle
Mixtape. I was giving an aggressive expression of revolt
and it was all coming together, I took one of the songs I
recorded with Bang Em and Domination and placed it on
the project. I had a lot of respect and love for Bang Em for
giving me insight and now the streets of D.C. and the world
would hear what we had dropped in the studio on the song
"What The Deal."

While putting together the CD, I had a premonition
come to me about a song. It was always a dream of mine
to meet Tupac, but now that I was going strong with my
rap career, it was a fantasy and constant thought of what
it would be like to actually do a song with Pac. The Pop Off
set the stage for it to become a reality. So I found a track
from Tupac and remixed it with a verse with me on it. The
song was entitled "Never Be Peace," and it was the perfect
fit to the Pop Off and the state of mind of a righteous
soldier rebelling against injustice. The CD was filled with
thirteen tracks and it was ready to be released. As we

finished, a producer that worked with the twins named Joke Dog asked could he give me a track for the Pop Off. Joke Dog was a white boy who made aggressive type beats, he was a good friend of the twins and a fan of my music. So I agreed to it and picked out one of his tracks and made a song called "Ryda." What was funny about Joke Dog was that every song he would hear of mine he would say the same thing, "I like this song Shyst this is the best one I've heard." I would smile and tell the twins, "He says the same thing about all of my songs, but I like how he keeps me inspired to get better." When Joke Dog heard "Ryda" he swore up and down it was my best song yet, so with that song being done, I wrapped up the CD and got it ready to be released.

When the recording was done it was on to making a cover for the project so it could be released to the street. I had an idea of a cover in the form of a motion picture and that's the direction I went with it. With all the other CD's and projects I had done up to this point I gathered everyone's opinion on it, but with this particular mixtape it was my baby and I let my heart lead me into its release. Even though I was creatively coming with all the ideas of the mixtape, my producers helped me with every aspect of it to see it through. Anton pulled out a camera and he took the pictures I wanted for the front and back cover and then we sat down and created the cover work. What came out was what I imagined it to be and now it was ready. I had the inserts printed and CD's burned to hit the streets and release it. Once the CD was released it had an effect on people I imagined it would and even greater, the streets embraced it to the point of everybody wanted their own copy. What was a common thing that became funny to me about the Pop Off was that people would buy it and then say at some point that someone stole it out of their car or took it out of their CD player. I burned over five thousand copies of the CD and as I did shows and traveled from D.C., Maryland, and Virginia, I sold them out of my trunk. I would have people tell me that they saw the CD for sale at local flea markets and I had no idea how they got there. At first, it bothered me, but as a few months passed by I realized that with good music people copying and bootlegging was a part of the game that turned out to be a compliment. Along with hearing the testimony of how people loved the CD, I would get real stories from the streets, stories that sometimes made me realize how powerful my influence was to people who listened. One day in a conversation with a good friend of mine, he told me how after the club one night he and his partners had got into an altercation with a rival crew they had problems with. As they left the club playing my Pop Off CD, it got them hype to the point that they did a drive-by while listening to my CD. The details of what happened he didn't go into, but the fact that it happened made me think a lot about what I had done with releasing this CD.

With The Pop Off buzzing in the streets, it gave me every avenue to network with DJ's and other artists. It became my business card to advertise my craft, and now that it was spreading out I put my mind on getting a few songs played on the local radio stations in D.C. The first DJ I reached out to was DJ Celo, Celo was a real hardcore DJ that spun on WPGC 95.5 at the time, he would be on the radio dropping bomb sound effects and talking trash to the whole city while he was doing it. Celo was famous for saying he plays what he wants, so I got his info and reached out to him and invited him to the studio to get him The Pop Off. Celo came through and showed love. I liked

Celo because when he came to the studio, he was in a two-door Cadillac CTS with tinted windows. So when the car pulled up, it just sat there for about twenty minutes in front of the studio and you could smell weed coming out the car. I was inside working, but it startled the twins, they asked me if I knew whose car it was and I said Nah. I could see it shook them up a little bit, so I went outside and looked in the car and sure enough, it was DJ Celo. He rolled down his window and nothing, but smoke came out, with a smile on his face. He came in and kicked it for a minute and he ended up playing one of the remixes from *The Pop Off* a few nights later on the radio.

With 95.5 under the belt with a spin, I reached out to another DJ named Alizay who was spinning on WKYS 93.9 in D.C. DJ Alizay was a good DJ and if I could get him to rock with it, it would be a good look. I had Alizay's number from bumping into him in the club, so I called him up and invited him to come down to the studio to check out the mixtape. Alizay was also into making beats so I told him I would hook him up with the twins and they could help him with whatever he needed. The thing I liked about Alizay has he always kept it cool with me and helped me *stay in good spirits. A few days later Alizay stopped through the studio for a meeting and a sit-down. He came in and we went into the beat making room and got straight to it, we played the CD from the top and he was all in it with smiles. We stopped the CD and Alizay looks over at me and was like "My nigga that shit fire." I was relieved when I heard his reaction and I asked him, "So it can get some spin?" He was like, "Nigga I'm a play it," I was like when? He said "Tomorrow" and we all busted out in laughter in the studio because he was letting me know it was a go and he was down. After we kicked it for a few, I had some other things that I needed to do, so I told Alizay I'll be listening tomorrow and I left him at the studio with the twins as they talked about beat making stuff. The next day on 93.9 during the rush hour mix, my remix to R Kelly's song "Hotel," came on the air. My voice sounded good on-air and I was praying this was going to kick off a big buzz for me and really pop off. Getting a few spins got me the awareness, but I learned that I needed to continue pushing records and being consistent. I later learned a lot from my mistakes, but the Pop Off was off to a good push with its release.*

CHAPTER 9

THE POP OFF 2

STILL SHOOTING

(COLOSSIANS 1:23)

If you continue in your faith, established and firm, and do not move from the hope held out in the gospel. This is the gospel that you heard and that has been proclaimed to every creature under heaven, and of which I have become a servant.

With the success of the Pop Off things started coming together for me as an artist. The Struggle Mixtape being in retail stores on consignment, I had visual awareness of storefronts throughout D.C., Maryland, and Virginia. After a year of being released, The Pop Off gave me even more visibility on mixtape shelves, but it brought my awareness to the street up another level. One of the things that a mixtape does is it can broaden your fan base if you use it correctly. The three songs I had done with Bang Em and Domination were now floating through New York on their series of mixtapes called Ground Work. The GroundWork was buzzing in New York because of Bang Em and 50 cents break up from G Unit. Bang Em started his own movement called Silverback Gorillaz and he was pushing them in New York hard to get them a deal. Bang Em would always invite me up to New York when they had events and I would go up and he would give me the realist experiences a soldier could get. The first time I went up they had just released another volume of Groundwork and the whole crew met up at Justin's, which was Puffy's restaurant. I had been there before, but this time was different. This time I was with Bang Em and his crew from South Side Jamaica Queens. That night a lot of celebrities came out to support Bang Em. One person, in particular, was Fredro Starr. I grew up listening to Onyx and I was a big fan of his films. This was my first time seeing him since our initial encounter in L.A. some time back. We chopped it up for a few and then he went to a table to sit and eat with this white girl that was with him. I liked how he rolled because it was just him and a girl with no security or anything. You could tell he was a real street nigga and not on no Hollywood shit. So as we all kicked it at Justin's, I went over and sat down at his table and chopped it up with him. Fredro treated me like family, as I sat with him I told him how much his music influenced me when I was younger and how it was a pleasure to meet him. He kept it chill and offered to buy me something to eat, but I kept it cool and just sat for a minute then left the table. It was those experiences in New York that helped me see the game clearer.

Clear enough that I was aware that a mixtape could spark major awareness, the awareness to the street was what I needed from the Pop Off and it brought back the return of the streets. What I mean by that is, in the street once they see your success, you get embraced, but once you get embraced you have to be prepared to deal with the hate. I say hate because it comes from jealousy and envy of what is seen as a success from someone with less ambition to acquire what you have given the effort to do. This part of life I dealt with in the street accordingly and effectively, but now it would come at me from another direction. One of the first things I did with the success of the Pop Off was formed, my team and crew. With leading my movement, I formed my own crew of rappers and entourage and called it Strugglaz Entertainment, and my artists were called the Strugglaz Click. My crew was a few of my cousins that rapped and the niggas that I made money with in the street that were real solid soldiers that had the credibility of being thorough. When I performed at shows we would show up twenty deep, when I had appearances, I was sure to have shooters with me. I took the insight of Bang Em Smurf and what he had done with G Unit and I embodied it in D.C., and it was growing strong.

One night I was at my studio outside parked in my truck with three of my niggas and we were smoking weed and kicking it as I would normally do at my studio at the end of my day. As I looked down at my phone in the middle of the conversation, I saw that I had a missed call, but what was strange is that my phone never rang. So on my phone, it said missed a call and it notified me of a new voice mail. For some reason, I felt a strange vibe because I know my phone didn't ring, so I had a look of skepticism on my face as if I were figuring out an unsolved mystery. I proceeded to playback the message and to my disbelief, it was a long voicemail from someone I never even met before. The voice on the message left a long rant on how he had heard the Pop Off and thought it was trash and blah blah blah. After his comments, this obvious hater proceeded to say that I would never make it and that "I was going nowhere." Then this fool had the nerve to leave his rap name and hung the phone up. While I was listening to this message my heart rate increased and I became furious and angry. My partners in the truck with me was looking at me because they could tell I was mad and when I got mad, my crew got mad, and when we all were mad things went my way, wrong or right. Before I could hang up everyone in the truck was like "What's up with it Shyst?" I went into a fury to them about the message on my phone, then I went into the studio and started raging about it so hard that everyone was like "Somebody doesn't know who they fucked with." It was obvious this rapper wanted my attention and I wasn't going to give it to him in a rap. I could tell by his accent on the phone he was from New York and I called the number back, but got no answer. I really wanted to do harm to him at that time and teach him a lesson. The next day I made a few calls and backtracked to find out who this kid was. I kept calling his number back, but would never get an answer. I knew I had flyers with my contact info on it at P.A. Palace in Forestville mall and I figured that's how he got my number. I started

doing my homework on this clown and after telling my
man Kal about it, he told me to give him a few minutes.
Kal called me back in about twenty minutes later and I had
this kid's whole resume in one day. He was a no-name
from New York staying with his baby mother at her house
in Maryland. I knew what hood he was in and what street
he was on. I gave him another call and when he didn't pick
up I kindly left him a nice message letting him know I found
him and his whereabouts and that I'd be catching up with
him just to let him know he played with the wrong one. In
about ten minutes of me leaving him a message, his
number pops back up on my phone, so I picked up to hear a
young humbled voice telling me how much he liked my CD
and that he didn't mean anything by it. I humbly told him
that he shouldn't have done it because it could have gotten
out of hand because I live a combat type of life. I let him
know it was cool and I'd let it rest and I would let him off
the hook with this because a lot of people was looking for
him. When I calmed down after getting off the phone with
him and had a chance to think clearly, what came to my
mind was a song to expose this clown and hurt him
without killing him. I'd do that by embarrassing him and

making him ashamed of entering into my lane. The whole situation gave me the spark and energy to go into the studio and start on The Pop Off 2, "Still Shooting." The first song on the CD was called "Glory" feat Biggie Smalls. The song starts off with the message from the previously mentioned hating rapper, I knew this would embarrass and expose him. Not only that, it would let my listeners know and understand how serious my competitiveness was in real life. To give balance, I took a Biggie Smalls beat and slaughtered it. Then to add insult to injury I left Biggie's verse on the track to enforce the state of mind when you're lyrically destroying a competing rapper.

While recording songs for the Pop Off 2 I wouldn't be in the studio as much because I would always be working in the street pushing and moving around. One day out of the blue I got a call from the studio and they asked me if I knew a rapper named Yukmouth and that he was there recording a song with a group of rappers from D.C. I remember when I was in Las Vegas with C-Bo and Bang Em that C-Bo had called Yukmouth on the phone and he was on the speaker saying he was in the UK and he wished he was there in Vegas. Yukmouth was a well-known rapper from California who was on the hit record "I Got Five On It." So for him to be at my studio was a big deal. When I got to the studio it was a mob of niggas in the lounge outside the recording room, and another group in the recording room with Yukmouth. So I kicked it in the lounge with the niggas Yukmouth had with him who happened to be my older homies from my hood, along with a few dudes from California. I waited until I knew they weren't recording and walked in the recording room and went straight to Yuk on the couch and introduced myself. I kept it so solid because we knew some of the same people C-Bo and Bang Em, so when I met him I let him know I was out in Vegas with C-Bo when they called him in the UK. As I spoke with Yuk he had this look on him like Ok, he affiliated. Yuk was receptive and genuine, so I left out the session and continued to kick it in the lounge with everybody until his session was over. As Yuk was leaving I stopped him and gave him the Pop Off 1, as he looked at it he was like "You got Bang Em and Domination on here?" We then swapped numbers as he left the studio. A few days went by and I got a call on my phone and it was Yukmouths number. When I picked up the phone Yuk was on one thousand, like "Yo its Yuk, I'm fuckin with you man, yo shit dope," I'll be back out there in a few months and we going to link up and get it. After getting off the phone with Yuk I felt like my vision was coming together and I was inspired to keep going strong with my process.

As I kept recording songs for the Pop Off 2 I had started thinking about what issues I could address that my listeners wanted to know about and hear. One of the biggest issues that every rapper or person who would hear me say is they thought I sounded like 50 cent. I never would let it get me mad and I would just say, "Nah 50 sound like me." Even though the comparison to 50 cent was innocent to most, it had started to be a hindrance to the greatness of my creativity. In reality, we just had similar voice tones. It wasn't like we rapped the same lyrics, but the comparison came up all the time and a lot of record executives passed on signing me because 50 cent had the biggest hit on the radio at the time, "In The Club," and was the biggest rapper in the game at the time. Most people who said it would discredit me in my mind as to say, you're good, but 50 cent got your sound. So with me dropping the Pop Off 2, I wanted to put a banger on it that would make everyone who heard it drop their jaw and say no he didn't. At this point, I never intentionally tried to sound like 50 cent, but with this record I did. I took the song where he destroyed Ja Rule and reversed it back at him to start controversy. I didn't have any personal issue with 50 cent, I actually admired his struggle because ours was similar, and it was his path that was taught to me by his best friend Bang Em. So you could actually say, he opened doors for me to be who I was and was going to become. This song wasn't really against him, it was a dis song meant for the listeners, to ultimately show the haters that I didn't fear crafting a diss track in a way that honestly only I could do. So I took his track called "Back Down," and shot at him with his own gun. It was one of the most brilliant things I had done at the time. I came out of the booth and everybody was saying, I need a copy of that. That's what I wanted and that's the level of creativity I brought to D.C. hip hop. The momentum of people becoming fans and wanting my new music was driving me to keep going. The 50 cent dis went through the roof and the streets were buzzing even before I could release the CD.

With the 50 cent dis on the Pop Off 2, I had a must-have CD already. Now I thought to myself, I'll put another track with me Bang Em Smurf and Domination on it, 50 cent's friend and now rival and that CD is gone, and that's what I did. We recorded a track called "Gangsta Travel" and now it was also on the CD, which made it a classic. I recorded altogether twenty-seven adrenalin rushed aggressive songs, and what came together was a true must-have classic. The Pop Off 2 Still Shooting left listeners excited about hip hop music in D.C. and is still relevant today.

CHAPTER 10

THE POP OFF 3

THE VOICE OF GOD

(ISAIAH 30:21)

Call to me and I will answer you and I will tell you great and hidden things that you have not known.

I put together a solid project and had one of the biggest diss records ever heard on it. Everyone saw my hunger and ambition, little ole me going to a big dog. Even though I was dropping hit records, I was still lacking an engine behind me that could push me to a label. That was the reason I would release these smash records that were recorded deal worthy on mixtapes, but unfortunately, it didn't pan out the way I thought it would. To be honest I knew I was in a lane by myself in D.C. and needed to just be heard by the right people. There was no other rapper or label at the time that could dominate the aura I embodied. I had the best producers in the city, with banging beats and I was making street money, so I was always good. The thing that kept me relevant was doing shows all throughout D.C., Maryland, and Virginia, so my fan base grew in time with my music. In the field of being an underground rapper, you are blessed if you have a mentor or someone to help you with situations. For me, I was more than blessed because Bang Em Smurf was who would help me through a lot of situations when I needed advice. As much as his situation with 50 cent was the gossip around him, he always remained a loyal soldier and I believe he was my biblical warrior assigned to help me along my path. There was a time at one of my shows and a fight broke out involving me and my entourage. At that moment I lost it and ended up getting into a shootout in the parking lot of the club. The next day I called Bang Em and told him because I felt like I needed to get away out of town and I needed someone that wasn't involved that I could talk to. He told me about how things were when he was with 50 cent and how their crew was always in those type of predicaments. He told me of stabbings at shows and the shootouts after. During that conversation he let me know that "If the niggas around me would let me be the one to shoot, stab and fight, then they don't need to be around you Shyst." Bang Em gave me rules to the game *that stuck with me and made me a stronger leader. As our conversation ended he let me know that he and Domination had gotten a distribution deal with Koch and he wanted me to come to New York to be with them as they took care of business. This for me was a blessing because Bang Em got his crew Silver Back Gorillaz a deal in about six months or so from flooding the market with their mixtapes, just as he had done while he was with G Unit. Koch at the time was where a lot of major industry rappers were releasing their music since they were known as the biggest independent distributor. For me, it was a chance of a lifetime to get a glimpse of the game up close in New York, so I took the trip by myself and went up there to handle business. Following the shooting at my show in D.C., I needed the getaway, mostly because I was paranoid about the aftermath of how many people were hit and if I would catch a charge from it. When I got to New York I met up with Domination in Queens and hopped in the car with them. Bang Em was taking care of some business, so he let me know he would meet up with me later that night and we would get together then while in New York I was treated not as a stranger, but as a family member, which* was a really good feeling. The love I got in New York from the streets was something I had never experienced prior to that point. It wasn't on any fairytale stuff, the realities were rough and serious, but the knowledge was an insight to me and gave me the necessary strength to lead a nation.

While taking frequent trips to New York, I would keep in touch with Yuk and my peoples out on the west. That's just what it was, even if you were underground and unsigned, you still needed to be plugged in across the coast to stay up and relevant. It was around this time when I got a call from Yukmouth telling me he had a show in D.C. and he would be out here in a week. Yuk was always good when he would touch down in D.C., he had connected with my older homies from my hood on 48th St. in North East, and that's who would take him through the city and hold him down while he was there. So it was a readymade situation with me, my true ties to the street and knowing solid people in the rap game was beneficial. Yuk was different when he touched down in D.C. this time, he was more amped up than before. He and his partner from Cali named Gonzo were stirred up the entire time. After Yuk's show, we all got up and kicked it to make a late-night movie and Yuk and Gonzo kept screaming The Game this and The Game that. I remember hearing them say, "He fucking with them G Unit niggas," after a while, it became obvious to me that something happened with The Game and Yukmouth out in Cali and they were now beefing and making diss songs at each other. I knew it was some west coast stuff I knew nothing about, so I kept my mouth closed about it and listened to them rap about it. The whole time they were going on, I'm quiet, but thinking in the back of my mind, "They going make me jump in this shit and set the whole thing off." I was thinking this jokingly in my mind because it was no way or reason for me to be on a Yukmouth diss against The Game. So after Yukmouth's show, we all wanted to take Yuk out in the city to see a Go-Go band called Backyard where we knew it would be popping. We decided to head out to a club called Aqua, a real hood club in D.C. We all met up at Aqua and we were about twenty people deep. It was all my childhood homies and older dudes who hustled in my hood with us and they all had Yuk's back like a mob. The night was cool and we all had a good time with Backyard, Yuk even went out on stage and rocked out with the band as they played, "I got five on it." Everything was good, but Yuk was from Cali and that night he had about $40,000 worth of jewelry on in the club. He was straight though all night, but when we were outside of the club, Yuk drifted away from the entourage talking with some girls. I had my eye on him and I started walking towards him and as I'm walking to him to secure him, I see a group of niggas looking at Yuk and his jewelry like it was dinner. They were plotting to make a move to snatch his jewelry, so I made my way close to Yuk to let them know he was covered and that got the attention of everyone that was with us. Once the niggas said something our entourage began arguing with them and I sprinted off to my truck like Jerry Rice to get to my gun. I got in my truck and pulled up in the street with my hand on my gun while they were holding Yuk back and arguing. I told them to get Yuk in here with me, so I opened my back door as they pushed Yuk in my truck and his niggas with him hopped in the truck with me. I had my gun in my hand and my hand in my lap as I drove us from in front of the club. The entourage of cars followed me and we headed back around our way. Once we pulled off,

Yuk and his folks were like, "Damn Shyst, you move fast as shit, you got us out that mother fucker, Holmes." I smiled with a smirk, but was serious when I told him, "We got you out here, you good." While I was driving Yuk back to his hotel the conversation with them was still on Yukmouth's beef with The Game. So Yuk yells out, "I need a studio and that breathe beat by fabulous." I told him we could hit my studio in the morning and I had the beat for him. Yuk got excited and agreed that we would hit the studio tomorrow, so he can record a diss against The Game. At this point, I was simply doing my duty to take care of Yuk while he was in town and thinking nothing of it. It's just what we did as loyal men in the element of street niggas and the rap game. When I was in New York, I was good, when I was in Cali, I was good and vice versa. When my folks came to D.C., I was there to hold them down. We met at my studio the next evening to get Yuk in the booth. Once we were all in the studio the energy was real. Yuk had the energy of Tupac on Deathrow, he kept going on about how this to diss was going to be big, how it was going to change the game. As he kept on, I started thinking how if I was on this track that I would blow upon it. How I could make a stand

and ride for Bang Em and we could get things popping. So Yuk dropped a verse on the diss track and his partner Gonzo laid a second verse on it. While they were recording I had written this hook in my head just playing around on the beat. When the song was done, Yukmouth looks over at me and says "Yo Shyst, you got a hook?" I jump at the opportunity like "Yeah for sure," I went into the booth and laid my hook. When I came out the booth the whole session was going crazy, Yuk kept saying, "You killed that shit." When I listened back to what I had done, I was in awe and taken back because this was something big and I could have never imagined being part of it. We wrapped up the session and started getting ready to leave the studio. As we were leaving Yuk says "Shyst we gone get together tomorrow and shoot the video to the song, this shit went be big my nigga." We left and I went my way and Yuk stayed another day in D.C. with my homies. I remember thinking to myself that this song was going to make some noise and be big in hip hop. The following day Yuk hit my phone and told me to meet him in my hood. When I got to my street where they were filming it was like a block party out there. It was people and kids everywhere *like I had never seen in my hood before. They had already*

shot a few scenes in the hotel and now it was time to put it

down on camera. With no ironed out plan we all decided

to put together our thoughts and started recording.

Yukmouth's diss on the Game was like no other, we had

one of our homies dress up in a pink G Unit outfit with a

pink bandana and get chased and beat up in the hood.

Along with it being a serious diss song the visual brought

humor to it while we were filming Yuk would always put

me in the center of the action. He let everyone know how

much he fucked with me and how close he was with me.

The cops came through to stop our shoot, but we just kept

getting footage until it was done. As the nightfall caught

up we wrapped up the video shoot and the director named

Funk kept saying, "This shit gone be out tomorrow." He

and Yuk kept huddling and Yuk would say, "This shit gone

be crazy." The next day Yuk released the video and it

spread like a wildfire. The video got over a million views in

a few days and everyone in the rap game was paying

attention. The feature on that song got me buzzing across

the country and now I was deep in the rap beef and it was

on. What was now a story from the outside looking in,

became the complete opposite in a short amount of time.
While the song I was on with Yukmouth was buzzing in hip
hop, it brought a lot of local attention to me as a rapper.
With me on that song dissing The Game and The Game
with G Unit and everything else, I was on high alert every
day. I was turned up before all this, but now I was on full
throttle twenty-four-seven, I was expecting anything all the
time. I kept two pistols on me, one for me and one for
whoever I had with me. See everybody in D.C. thought I
had signed to Yuk and I had a deal, but Yuk was just
helping me in the game. He gave me an opportunity and I
went in with him. At the same time though a lot of Dj's
and radio stations in D.C. looked at me as the bad guy of
D.C. and no one wanted to be part of me or even support
the fight I was in. Things got real on the west coast when
some crips tried to jump Yuk in the club and they snatched
his chain. I stayed in touch with Yuk and we kept things in
perspective with my career. I know he had an open door
for me, but I knew I had to stay in D.C. and keep building.
Eventually, The Game and Yukmouth's Beef made it on the
Beef 3 DVD that was out and it was playing on BET for a
minute. I was still pushing The Pop Off 2 and grinding in

the street. Eventually, Yuk and The Game squashed their beef and things moved on.

When The Game released his debut album, he came to do promo for it in D.C. and me being me I wanted to get at him to let him know I could get to him. Not in a way that would bring harm to him, but let him know that in D.C., he was an easy target I could get to. I knew the security at the store he was doing a signing at and he snuck me in and I was able to meet The Game face to face. I said my peace with him and we left it at that. The next week The Game left G Unit, I heard it was because 50 heard he had squashed a beef in D.C. I used to wonder was he referring to me and The Game. With everything I had going on, I was still on the road traveling heavy. I got invited to perform with Bang Em and Domination at Club Speed in New York, this was big for me because this was my first time performing in New York. Speed was a hood spot that only serious street artist performed at, Bang Em would always extend his hand to me and we were more of brothers in the struggle at this time. When I met up with Bang Em in Queens for the show, it was nothing short of what the world would see on TV when he was with G Unit.

It was about thirty goons outside his house as we got ready to head to the club while we were at Bang Em's house, he got a call and on the other end was someone letting him know 50 cent was in New York at BBQ's. So Bang Em hung up the phone and jokingly says, "See this nigga don't know if I want him, I could have him," and then laughed. Bang Em never really wanted to hurt 50, but these were two friends of combat in the street, so they respected each other as street niggas and took precaution with their feud. When I found out that 50 was in town, it put things into a more serious perspective because he and Bang Em were not just rap dissing, it was physical and a real war zone in New York between them. Bang Em was a real strategic dude though, so as we all gathered to leave for the show, two limousines pulled up outside, one for the entourage and the other was empty and a lure. The empty limousine was there just in case anyone tried to shoot up the limo they would be hitting an empty vehicle. Bang em and Domination followed in an SUV behind both limos, and that's where I was in the SUV with Bang Em and Domination. Bang Em would keep me close and he made sure I was always in good hands and was well respected when he was around. We pulled up to Speed and the club was packed. It was a line outside the club and police everywhere to secure the crowd. As we pulled up, I remember Bang Em getting excited because people came out and it was a good look. When we went in it was jammed packed in the club, we were deep and we had two armed shooters in the club with us. A lot of people showed to support Bang Em, one of them being Fredro Starr from Onyx. I saw him and it was a good look because all eyes were on Bang Em and Domination in the club and we were about to go on stage. As we headed downstairs, the club was packed with blood and crips from New York and people from every borough. We went on stage and rocked it. My verse from the song we did came on and as I started rapping it, the crowd became more hype. What made it even better for me was that while I was rapping I looked to my left and Fredro Starr was standing next to me on stage with the biggest smile, rocking from side to side with me as I rapped. For me, this was a moment I was grateful to God for. I remember being a fan of Onyx and seeing Fredro on stage at a show and now I'm on stage with him and I'm rapping, it was like a dream come true. We left the club and headed back to Queens that night and as we came to a stoplight, a car was slowly pulling up next to our SUV. Once Bang Em saw it he yelled out "Yo who the fuck is this?" At the time Bang Em didn't know I had my gun on me, but I did. So when the car pulled up I whipped out and was leaning on the door to shoot out the window, so Bang Em was like "Yo let me see that shit Shyst." I handed the gun to him and we were ready to fire on the car, but just then the car made a right turn and we could see they were just civilians driving. We all bust out laughing and joking because Bang Em didn't know I was strapped and they liked how I moved with them. We got back to Queens and I jumped in my car and came back to D.C. that night.

Back in D.C., it was like moving in a time warp where we were behind time. It was like I'm shaking and moving in the rap industry and waiting for my city to catch up to me. Everywhere I went it was a million questions from people who knew I was buzzing and wanted to know what was going on with me. Some thought I was signed to Yukmouth and some thought I was with Bang Em. A lot of people just referred to me as beefing with 50 cent, something I was tired of hearing, but I knew I could use the controversy to keep me relevant in people's minds. In reality, I was still trying to get a deal or a situation that I could get paid and take care of my family. I was still selling drugs in the street and still living a life of violence. It made for good material, but it put me at risk of the dangers of the streets, and with the dangers of the street, it's jail or death. So after a year of pushing the Pop Off 2, I wanted to reinvent myself and drop a relevant project that would answer all the questions that were surfacing. I put together a plan and I did just that. I started working on the Pop Off 3 and called it, The Voice of God. I titled it, The Voice of God because I wanted the listeners and my followers to know where my strength and source came from. Once I got started recording it, it was like painting a masterpiece of work. I made it like it was an interview and I was giving the answers to the questions that I was asked in the streets. I unleashed several new tracks, including one with Yukmouth, Domination and I together on the same record, along with The Game and Yukmouth's diss song. This mixtape was and still is a classic in D.C. hip hop that helped me bring the real essence of gangster rap to D.C.

CHAPTER 11

DEAL WITH THE DEVIL

(MATTHEW 4:1)

Then Jesus was led by the spirit into the wilderness to be tempted by the Devil.

    While recording The Pop Off 3, I was pushing hard with recording and making things happen to stay on top of my game with my music. The twins as producers were always trying to get a production deal and get signed as producers and work in the music industry, that was their dream from the time I met them, and it was no different now. My goal with every mixtape we put out was to give display to my work and their production and it always prevailed. We were a great fit as artists. The twins and Pops were always having meetings and appointments with people in the industry to shop their beats and shop the artists they produced, me being one of those artists. So during the time I started working on The Pop Off 3, they met a manager and entertainment lawyer by the name of Everett. Everett was from Philly and managed the rapper

Cassidy at the time. I never got involved with the people the twins and Pops were dealing with too much, I just did what I had to do in the studio. With Everett, it was serious though after he heard their beats and the music they were making he wanted to help them get a deal. I had a few meetings where I met Everett and had a chance to talk to him. He was very encouraging to me and I could tell he believed in me and that I had what it took to be the artist to take D.C. hip hop to the next level. He would always mention to me about his nephew from Philly named Meek Mill and how he wanted us to do something together. I agreed to do it and I always took his advice on my direction. A few weeks went by and Everett and the twins along with Pops had a big meeting in New York. Normally they would take me on out of town trips, but this time they took Pops and went up and had their meeting. When they came back from New York they were excited and the first thing they told me was that "They're trying to sign you Marc." One would think me getting signed should have been good news, but what Pop and the twins would say is, if I sign they would put me with industry producers and I'll be gone and the label wouldn't work with them. I didn't *see it that way though, I was like if I'm in then we all in. That's how we would get in the game and big. I kept working on my mixtape and record, but now the mood was different. I couldn't tell what it was, but when they came back from New York their lack of interest with me as an artist and their ambition to work with me was gone. I would come to the studio and record and it would be all business and standoffish now. I thought it would be our time, but something was different. I came in the studio one day to record, and Anthony let me know they were going to be going to Cali because they felt D.C. wasn't working for them at that point and they felt Cali was where they could go and get on. I felt like something was weird about all this, I had to disagree and let them know I'm staying here. I would ask them what happened with the deal with Everett and they would push it off like "Aww it's nothing, we don't need the man, let's go to Cali, and we can get on." I wasn't buying it though, I knew something wasn't right and I had to prepare myself to survive. The twins helped me put together The Pop Off 3 and then they all relocated to California while I stayed in D.C. The new change was difficult for me at first because I couldn't believe what I was seeing manifest, and if it was what I thought it was, then I had to let it be. This was the first time in years that I didn't have a studio home and a team to work with. I felt like they dropped my deal in New York, and it was just too much for them. They couldn't get a deal with me with all my controversy and gossip and just didn't want to work with me anymore. No matter whatever the case was, I knew I had enough material to make it. I believed in myself and I knew it was time to grow and get to the next level. Just like all the other times in my life on my journey, and I recognized the moment. When I stayed in the streets I kept pushing my music, but I was in the street a lot more. Two months after they left I caught a gun charge in D.C. and with catching a charge it was a lot of people who faded because of my trouble. I found myself in a black ball state with nothing, but my faith to make it out with what I knew was going to work. I ended up getting the charge none papered due to my fight of illegal search and it worked. I knew what I was talking about and when my lawyer argued it, it was dropped. See they didn't have a true reason to search me and they racially profiled me, so the charges were dropped.*

While I continued to do shows and push my CD's, I was out one night and when I finished performing I had my CD's in the club with my crew selling them. As I stood at the bar, a guy approached me and told me he wanted to buy my CD's, I point him in the direction of where to go and he bought two of them, The Pop Off 2 and The Pop Off 3. After he bought the CD's he came back to me and asked could I sign them for him, he told me his name was Rico and he let me know he liked my performance. I was honored by his compliment and support and talked with him for a minute. He mentioned that he did some management and might be able to help me if I needed it. We switched numbers and that was that, nothing new to me. I would always meet people while out and about, so a week went by and I got a call from Rico. As he was on the phone he was excited about the CD's he bought, I could tell he was really into them. He mentioned to me all the stuff he was working on, and how he would love to be on my team and work for me. I didn't agree to work with him at first, I needed to see if he was official or just talking well. So I stayed in touch with him on and off for a few weeks until we met back up. The next time I saw Rico he wanted *to meet up and let me know what he could do for me. Rico was cool, but he was an over the top type of guy, you know he talked big money, but was broke. He had a lot of ideas, but that's what they were, just ideas. He hadn't really done anything in the game to be a manager, but he loved my music and I knew he believed I was going to make it big. He mentioned he had connects to the music industry and he wanted to help me get a deal. I wasn't interested in him managing me, but I liked his over the top approach because while he was around me he let everybody know that I was the King from D.C. and the next big thing. Rico was kind of crazy too, he was always ready to shoot some shit up and I liked that about him because he was always thinking like how I was thinking as far as securing me. I told Rico to see what he could get shaking and create some opportunities and we would take it how it came. He was excited I gave him a chance and he was on his job. The next day Rico called me up on one hundred like normal, telling me he had someone he wanted me to meet. He wanted me to meet his partner Troy who used to work for Jay Z and Rocafella. He said Troy heard my music that he sent him and loved it. Rico set us up on a call, we all met* up and had a sit-down. Troy was a Muslim as was Rico, so they viewed things the same way on a lot of things. Troy was an older guy who would look like your uncle that went to Harvard and is a lawyer now. Troy had on a full dress suit and tie and he knew his business. Troy really was tied to Rocafella and had done some marketing for them prior, so he had good relationships there. Troy had the connections in New York with a few labels and he knew how to move in the record industry. Troy let me know he loved my music and wanted to push it to a few people and get me a deal. He let me know we could proceed from there with business, and as a rapper trying to get on I was with it. Troy's view on things was he wanted to start a bidding war, that's when a talented artist has a group of labels who have the interest to sign them and they start competing with the highest salary to get the artist to sign. I was cool with it, so when the meeting was over I gave Troy a CD with my unreleased material on it. He said he would listen to it and start pushing me to see what we could do. After we met we all would stay in touch on the phone daily to stay on schedule with our plan. All Troy needed me and Rico to do was stay busy with shows until *we got a deal and we did just that. Rico was excited even more because he saw things coming together for me and the vision of me getting a big record deal. For me, it wasn't about the money moreso, it was the true essence of me making it to the top where I was destined to be. Rico saw it that way too, he used to always tell me "It's prophecy, you the one Shyst." See by now I had read the whole entire bible once and was reading it for a second time. So I understood my calling and I believed in Gods Son Jesus and his life so much that I understood prophecy. I was proud of Rico, see no one ever really believed in his ideas of managing or that he knew the music business. A lot of people didn't do business with Rico because he was over the top, but with representing me he had something that was giving him power and leverage. I was proud of him because that's why I gave him a chance and it was all happening while Troy was doing what he was doing. Rico would reach out and get me involved with anything he could to be of help to me. He set me up a show once in D.C. with Blackmen Magazine. It was a swimsuit competition at a club called Zanzibar. This was big, Rico set it up for me to perform at the competition. I can* honestly say that this show broke me into the rap game. When we got there I had Rico escorting me around like I was famous and people could notice it too. At the show, it was over one hundred beautiful models in swimsuits competing. The thing about it was, you could see four or five beautiful women at one time in a club, but in a room with over one hundred models in swimsuits, you got to be solid or it will break you. I played it cool the whole time that night, I understood the business and my conduct ever more after that night because of being exposed to that. You could tell everyone wanted to know who I was and where I was seated was where all the models were in the middle of the action. So it was obvious I was somebody and an entertainer. At first, it was overwhelming to play the excitement off, but after a moment my mind switched and I realized this was my calling and this was what I was sent to do. When I absorbed it, I was comfortable in it, I was so cool with it that a lady in the club that night called me over to her and asked for my number. When Rico and everyone saw it, they loved it and they knew I had it. See Rico and everybody with us wanted to see how people would react and how I would react to this environment, and when the lady had to have me I knew I was a gold mine and I had the glow to make it. I performed that night and we continued to stay pushing in the streets. About a week went past and Troy got back to us and wanted us all to meet up because he had some news for us. By this time a lot of my partners and crew knew I was close to a deal and we were all waiting to see what was next for me. We all met downtown on U St. across from Bens Chili Bowl to talk business. Once there, Rico, Troy and I sat down and went over everything. Troy told me he had a situation for me, he had sent my music to his friend and business partner in New York by the name of Tom Whapels. Tom's daughter was Tracy Whapels and Tracy had worked at Bad Boy with Puffy for years and now she was working at Def Jam under Jay Z. Troy let me know that Tom loved my music and that he would walk me through to get a deal. It was going to be either Bad Boy or Def Jam, and there it was, I finally got to a situation where I was about to get signed and live out my dreams and vision. We all left the meeting that night excited about what was in store for me. This was about to be big for D.C., a rapper signed to a major deal that could put the city on. There were a few rappers in D.C. that were making noise far as radio and TV, but no one at this point had that major look like this. In a way, I was just grateful to God for always leading me through my struggle and keeping me in hopeful situations. I kept quiet about it and just got mentally ready. Rico and I would talk for hours on how it was going to be. The chance to make a difference, the chance to be great in hip hop. In all the anticipation two days went past and Rico and I got a call from Troy saying that Tom Whaples passed away from a heart attack. The news devastated us all. I could tell by the way Troy spoke of Tom that he was a great man. A person who could just get things done, Tom wasn't involved in the music business to my knowledge, he just believed in my music and he was going to get me a deal done with his daughter Tracy. It was a position of grace, but with Tom passing away, it all went down the drain. See Tom never got a chance to present my music to his daughter Tracy before he died, she never knew of it. Rico and I would say to Troy, why he doesn't just tell Tracy the story, Troy said he would and we hoped he could make the connection, so I could get the deal while Tom's burial was being put together, Troy mentioned to me that he may be able to get me to his funeral, but he emphasized maybe and let me know it was no guarantee. I took it for what it was and was trying to see what God was doing. I knew this was a great opportunity and I felt like Toms death was something aligned in God's plan and I tried to see the good in it and not the negative. I knew that Mr. Tom Whapels was a great man, and I was blessed that my music inspired him to work with me. I felt like my music moved on with Tom, me being one of the last things he was working on before he died. I felt my music went on to heaven with Tom and it was going to be in God's hands now, that's how I saw it and I am forever grateful for Mr. Tom Whaple's soul. A week went by and Troy calls me up out the blue like, "Marc, Tom's funeral is today and I'm a take you with me if you want to go." He told me that JayZ and Puffy maybe there, he didn't know for sure. Now in the back of my mind, I was a little skeptical on going because I didn't want to attend to see if Puffy and Jay Z would be there, but I wanted to pay my respect to Tom and pray that his daughter would work with me or lead me in the right way. So I went to pay respect and see if it was what Tom led it to be. For reasons unknown to me, Tom's funeral was right here in the DMV in Alexandria VA, ten minutes from D.C. The church that held Tom's funeral was right in our back yard and his family and friends would be traveling down here for his home going. So I put it in God's hands and I went and picked up Rico and Troy and drove us to Tom's funeral. When we got there, there was an awkward since of silence toward Troy from people there. As we stepped in the doorway of the funeral home I saw Tracy Whaple's coming down the hallway toward us. When I saw her I remembered her face from TV, like making the band and being with Puffy. When Tracy walked by us Troy spoke with her briefly, but you could tell she wasn't in the mood to converse as she was burying her father. Troy let me know he would talk with her later when he could, so we went outside to the front of the church to wait for the service to start and for the rest of the family to arrive. About fifteen minutes went by and a black Cadillac SUV pulls up and out appears Puffy with a team of his staff. When I saw him I was in awe and I was taken by the sureness of this moment. With all of that going on in my head, ten minutes later as we were still in front the church a black van followed by an SUV pulls up and out of the van hopped Jay Z. I remember thinking this is the closest I've ever been to people of this nature without it being chaos. Jay Z and Puffy were friends of Tom and his family, so it wasn't a big deal to anyone there, it was normal to them, but not to me. I was trying to figure out how all this could be in my lap and what I needed to do to take advantage of what Tom had left me. All this happened while Troy, Rico and I were in the front of the church conversing, that's where everyone was waiting for the funeral to start. As we talked, Puffy and Jay Z were standing next to us about three feet away talking. Troy looks over at me and says "Yo Marc go head over and speak to them." I hadn't been nervous in years, but when he said that I didn't know what to do or even what to say that would be respectful to them and especially at a funeral. I hesitated for a moment and then I said, "Ok," I took a quick look to the left of me and when I looked back in front of me Rico and Troy were gone. I mean really like they disappeared into thin air. I knew they had gone into the church, but they moved fast. As I stood there, I could hear Jay Z and Puffy laughing and talking beside me. I took a deep breath and I took two steps over to them and introduced myself. It was the most *awkward introduction I ever was placed in, but I knew I*

had to talk direct and keep their attention. So I looked at

Jay Z and said that I commended him for squashing the

beef with Nas and that he killed a lot of demons when he

did that. Jay Z looked at me with a look like, ok you got

some insight. Then he said "I appreciate that" I let them

know I was an artist and I worked with Tom. While I was

talking I looked back around us and it was crazy because at

that moment it was Puffy, Jay Z and me in front the church

by ourselves, everyone else had gone into the church as the

funeral started. I looked at Jay and Puff and Puff held his

head down with a sneaky and boogie look while he chewed

on a toothpick, but Jay Z was fully attentive to me and

nodded his head and agreed with what I was saying. With

us being the only ones not inside the church I told them

both that it was an honor to meet them and I looked

forward to working with them soon. I shook both of their

hands and we went back inside to the funeral. While I was

walking to my seat at Toms funeral I was thinking to

myself that was a monumental moment in my life and I

was so thankful to God because who, but God could do this

and at his house of worship. I got to my seat next to Troy and Rico and I noticed that Jay Z sat two rows in front of me to the left. I kept staring at Jay Z because he was so close to me that it was ridiculous while I stared I kept thinking about how it would feel to be signed to him and that this could be a reality now. Jay Z was a megastar, but while the funeral was going on he kept playing with this little girl in front of him, sticking out his tongue at her as she kept ducking behind her seat laughing at him. All this while the funeral was going on, the little girl was about six or seven years old and it was amusing to see him in an unguarded state. As we were leaving the funeral I walked past Jay Z and told him peace and he nodded back and we left the funeral.

After the funeral, we stayed focused on our plan to get me a deal. Rico and I would always ask Troy did he ever talk with Tracy to see if she could help us. Troy would always brush it off and say no and that we would get a deal without her help. It seemed a little strange to me, but I trusted he knew what he was doing, so we kept pushing and moving forward. Troy eventually got me a meeting in New York with a manager who used to work with Jay Z named Big Face Gary. Big Face Gary worked with Jay Z and Dame Dash at Rocafellas at the height of their career. Along with meeting Gary, Troy wanted to meet with the lawyer he had working on my behalf named Peter Allen. Peter worked for a law firm named, The Marshall Firm and they represented the major artists in the music business. The day of our trip to New York we arrived early because we had two big meetings. The first meeting was with Big Face Gary at a studio in Manhattan. When we go to the studio, Troy called Gary and he let Troy know he was walking up to the studio. I looked up and saw Gary and I could remember him from various shows and it felt as if I was on TV with Rocafella. Gary walked us up to the studio and we went into a state of the art studio with big speakers. Troy and Gary spoke for a little and we got straight to business. Gary took the CD Troy gave him, which was my unreleased music and pressed play. Now up to this point, I had never heard my music that loud. When the first track came on Gary closed his eyes sat back in the seat and zoned out. After the first verse and the hook, he started the record over from the beginning, he opened his eyes and looked at me and said, "You good kid, this hot." Gary was an upfront dude and he told me, "If you were *wack, I would tell you, but I like your flow." So he started the song from the beginning and let the song finish. When the second song came on he did the same thing, he laid back in the chair closed his eyes and zoned out to it. Just as he did before, after the first verse and the hook, he started over from the beginning. He looked at me and asked me, "You ever think of cutting your hair?" I told him Nah, and he let me know if I cut my hair and had a clean-cut that I would kill the game and it would make me more marketable. I agreed that I would eventually do it and we continued with the meeting. Gary listened to a few more songs and he let Troy know he could get started with moving my music and get me buzzing in the industry. The buzz would bring us a deal and we could all get it done. With that meeting under our belt, we left the studio and went to Peter Allen's office. Once we were at Peter Allen's office we all sat down with Peter. Peter was your typical surfer looking white guy who looked like he knew nothing about rap music, but what Peter did know was the business of music and the music industry. Troy let Peter know that I had a couple people and labels interested and they were ready to get representation for me. Peter let*

Troy know the steps we would need to do to get my buzz up, so we could land a big deal. Peter told us he would put together a contract to represent me and we could make it happen. So we left New York with good momentum and ready to work to make my deal happen. All I had to do was just stay focused and that's what I did. A couple of days later I met up with Troy and Rico and I signed a deal with them. The agreement entitled them to some of my signing bonus and certain rights when I got a record deal. Some real encrypted plot of the money type of shit, with Peter Allen and The Marshall Firm's name all on it. See Rico played Troy's right hand through all this and Rico was being patient, but he was an aggressive over the top dude that thought street about every situation there was. Rico wanted Troy to call Tracy and make the deal happen, so we could get to the top. Troy wanted to make other moves and build me up to get a big deal offered to me. In the end, Rico wanted the money now and Troy wanted to get more. Their indifference and Rico's greed caused them to clash. Rico started back trailing Troy and getting in touch with the lawyer's office, Troy's wife and other contacts to stir stuff up. Rico started sending me emails about Troy and telling me how he was a fraud and bad businessman, how we need to fire him and just go and get my deal. What Rico wanted was control and I just wanted them to make a deal happen for me. While I'm hoping they would work it out and settle things, Rico was planning a move to get me a deal and get him the power. At the time I didn't see what he was doing, but now I know. What Rico did was call up a meeting at his house. Rico wanted to clear the air and wanted to have a discussion, that is what he told Troy. He told me he was going to let Troy know he was no longer needed and get him to sign a release paper on me. I didn't want to pick sides, I just wanted to get the deal done with the right person. What was going to happen I didn't know? The day of the meeting I could tell that something serious was happening in the spirit realm because as I'm driving to Rico's house to meet them, it started raining then the sun came out through the rain while it was still raining. Definitely a sign to me of what was happening. I got to Rico's house before Troy so he called Troy to see where he was, and he said about twenty minutes away. While we waited Rico told me that when Troy got there he was going to make him sign my release papers, so I could be free of him. Rico's plan was to just take me to the Paul Marshall Firm himself and get me a deal, a greedy move to gain power. I had a gut feeling that this was a bad idea on Rico's part, but he felt he knew what he was doing. When Troy got to his house we greeted and then we all sat in Rico's living room to talk. Troy looked as if he were coming from the mosque because he had a Muslim turban on his head. Rico starts out the whole meeting with "I think we need to move forward with Marc and get the deal and just get Marc gone, so what I'm a need you to do is sign this paper. "So then Troy starts talking with a laugh as if Rico was joking and says "Look Rico, I told you man, we were going to." Just then Rico jumps up pulls out his gun on Troy in the living room. When he pulled out the gun Troy's eyes got big like golf balls, but he stayed calm like he knew Rico would do something like this. Rico pulled out a form and with his gun pointed in Troy's face, made him release me from his contract. After he signed it Rico kicked him out. I stayed for a few minutes after, but I was just too uncomfortable with what just happened. Rico was talking and trying to carry on and laugh, but in my mind, I was like this dude *crazy and out of control. I left feeling like I don't know if that was the right thing or the worst thing that just happened. At the time it just didn't feel right, I felt like my life was a big mess and I had to figure my way out. That night that it all went down, I got a call from Troy. Troy wanted me to know he knew it wasn't my fault. He knew what Rico was doing and he knew Rico wanted to go to Peter Allen hoping to get a deal for me. Troy also knew that what Rico was trying to do wouldn't work. I said my peace with Troy and he said his peace with me. He let me know he was leaving the music business alone and getting out. He wished me luck and we parted ways. In the following days, Rico did just as Troy knew he would, he called and set up a meeting with him and I, but what Troy didn't know was that Rico wasn't meeting with Peter Allen, he had us set up to meet Mr. Paul Marshall, the big dog. See when Rico was calling up there to New York about my contract, he was calling and speaking with Mr. Marshall about it. This lead Mr. Marshall to want to see who this was that was causing a big stir up in his firm over a record deal. Rico tried to get me to sign some paper the day before we had the meeting, talking about this the right* deal. I looked at the paper and seen his name and company name all on it and said, Nah let's see what happens at this meeting in New York and we can go from there. By now I knew my leverage and I had to be smart. So Rico understood and agreed and we went up to New York back to The Marshall Law Firm. The day of the meeting we got there and sat in the waiting area and waited to see Mr. Marshall. After ten minutes went by I was thinking, damn is he alright back there? After about thirty minutes I went to the secretary and made sure he knew we were there. She went back into his office to notify him of our arrival, and came back out and said Mr. Marshall will see you now. When we got in his office he welcomed us and gave us a seat, as he sat and slowly rocked in his executive chair. Mr. Marshall was an older Jewish man with white-gray hair, sort of like an older Joe Pesci, a real mob type of guy. Mr. Marshall read us both from the time we came into his office. He knew Rico was the one leading me there, so he engaged in conversation with Rico the most. Mr. Marshall was old, so his voice was like a whisper, which meant you had to really listen to him and pay attention to hear what he was saying. Mr.

Marshall gave us a brief history of some things he did in the music industry. After he mentioned that he helped get reggae music to the United States I started daydreaming at the pictures on his wall. As I stared around his voice faded out low and all I could think was, "What is going on, and what is he going to say in the conversation that could get me on and am I at the right place." Right when I snapped back, I heard him say that Peter Allen no longer worked there. Peter had been released from the firm. Mr. Marshall then let Rico know that the contract that Peter drafted for Troy was never authorized by his firm and that it was a fraudulent contract. To sum it all up he let us know that there was nothing he could do for us. Mr. Marshall looked at me and told me to stay in touch, maybe some time down the line things might open up and he told me to keep working. After that meeting, I ended up fading away from Rico and walking in faith to find my way. The whole idea of obtaining a record deal had taken a lot out of me and I needed to rebuild again.

CHAPTER 12

THE POP OFF 4

2000SHYST

(DEUTERONOMY 31:6)

Be strong and courageous. Do not be afraid or terrified because of them, for the Lord your God goes with you; He will never leave nor forsake you.

By now in my walk with God, I was reading the bible for the second time. Now I'll admit that once I read the bible from Genesis to Revelation, I asked God what I should do next because I still felt compelled to seek him. When I sat in meditation I heard his spirit say, read it again. When I started reading it this go-round, I had more understanding of things I didn't know. When you think of not knowing it seems like a place of fear, a place of giving up. Not with God though, God puts us in unknown spaces, so that you can trust his will for your life. At this point, I had seen things go from bad to good and back to being bad. I was confused as to why sometimes, but I kept my faith, I kept the vision that I knew God had placed in my heart and I continued to move forward. With the separation from the twins and now the confusion between Rico and Troy, I was back in the place of looking for hope in the game. I would spend time with my family and kids as much as possible while still moving in the streets. I kept my crew and team strong by staying in the mix with shows and pushing The Pop Off mixtapes. I still had The Struggle Mixtape in stores and Vision Coming True that was unreleased. I would see Rico still on Myspace and other social media platforms fronting like he was in the music business, but I just stayed away from him and his bad energy. The one thing that Troy told me about Rico after he pulled the gun on him was that Rico was a wild and aggressive guy that would fight until the death if you needed him too. He also said that he wasn't smart, because, with guys like that, a smart guy would always win because he could easily find another wild and crazy guy that could do the same thing. He advised me to just leave him be, keep things moving and keep my fan base growing, so that is what I did. It was 2005 and the Washington Wizards had just made it to the playoffs against the Chicago Bulls. With a home game in D.C., it was the perfect place to be downtown where everyone would be to push my mixtapes. My crew would always be with me because I had put them on songs that were on my mixtapes and we moved together to get people familiar with our brand. The night of the game as I was driving around the Wizard's arena to find parking for my SUV, I made a right turn on 7th St. and there was a police barricade to assist with the high flow of traffic in front the arena. When I approached the intersection an officer stepped out in the middle of the street and gestured his hand for me to stop. When I stopped, he walked up to my window, as he was approaching I realized that I had my handgun in the middle compartment and the handle of the gun was visible. The officer came to my window and said I had a headlight that was out and asked for my license and registration. While giving him my information I was trying to hold the compartment with my gun in it closed with my arm, but he could tell something was up. The officer looked back at a fellow officer and whispered something and then asked me to step out of the vehicle. I asked for what reason was I being pulled from my car and at this point he and his fellow officers proceeded to place their *hands on their weapons and said: "I'm not going to ask you again sir, step out of the vehicle." I knew it could get worse than what it was so I stepped out. When I got out, my partner Tom stayed in the passenger seat and they looked in and found my weapon and put me in cuffs. I could tell Tom was scared and I saw him deny he knew anything about it and they let him go. I had this feeling as he walked off carefree that he wasn't as loyal as I thought and now I'm in cuffs he figured I was done. With the handcuffs on me, the police put me in the back of a squad car and kept me there until the game was over. Fifteen minutes went by and they put another young black guy in the car with me who they just found weed in his car. This guy was trying to talk to me, but I was numb to it all and didn't have anything to say to him. I felt like my life was over and I had lost everything at that moment. It was the worst feeling I could imagine, so in a spiritual rage, I started talking to God in front everybody around. I yelled up to God that I was doing what he sent me to do. I told God I needed him to save me and that he was the only one I trusted and I asked that he save my life from this trouble I'm in. With tears in my eyes screaming at the top of my* lungs looking at the roof of the cop car, I cried out to God in the most realist conversation I ever had. The guy in the cop car with me got scared and never said another word again. When the cop finally got in the car and took me to the station, I was so relieved. I was ready to see how worst it was going to get next. As I road in the back seat on my way to the station, my spirit was dead. I couldn't believe this, it felt like being taken to my grave. We drove past the U.S. Capitol and I looked over at it like this some shit off a movie and one day the world will see what I'm seeing right now. We got to the jail and I was just ready to be buried. After sitting in a holding cell with about five other men for two hours, they finally called me out to the arresting officer. The officer then read me my rights and proceeded to get my information to fill out my arrest sheet. In this office there sat the arresting officer who told me to stop in the middle of the street. Along with him were three other officers who were out there at the time I was arrested. While the officer was asking my info, one of the officers said, "Whose music was that in the radio," I looked up at him with a surprised look like, "It was me, I'm a rapper." The officer then said, "Man you don't need to be out here

with guns, you need to be out here doing shows and stuff."
He was excited about my CD and it was crazy to me. The
arresting officer then looked at me and said, "You need to
just get you security, you can't have a gun." I jokingly told
him, "I don't have security, that's why I got a gun." The
officer let me know if I was in Maryland I could, but in D.C.,
the police were only allowed to carry a handgun at that
time. So I looked the officer in the eyes and I asked him,
"So for real what am I looking at for the gun?" He looked
at me and with no stress and like it was nothing asked me,
"You ever been arrested for a gun in D.C.?" I said "Nah,"
and he said, "You'll probably get probation." My face got
tight and with a serious look I said, "Stop playing with me."
He smiled and said, "Seriously if it's your first gun charge,
you'll be alright." They finished my paperwork and sent me
in a holding cell to be taken to the central cell to see the
judge in the morning. When I saw the judge the next
morning I had now been detained for about sixteen hours.
The judge called me up and set another date for me to
come back, letting me go on my own recognizance until my
preliminary date. I was in shock and I was grateful, I was
released from the jail and made it home. When I got home

I was drained, but at the same time feeling blessed to be free after thinking I would never see the light of day for a while.

I retained a court-appointed lawyer and argued the fact that the search was illegal because there was no reason or evidence of proper suspicion to search my truck. After two arraignments the charges were non papered, meaning set aside and could be brought back at a later time if needed. I got in a situation and God pulled me out. With the stress of my charge, I began to find other ways to progress to stay out of trouble and find my way back into music. I began to dig into my Bible more and did my best to go to church. About a month or so had passed and on one Sunday I took my daughter to church with me. I went to First Baptist Church of Glenarden and our church was always packed, you were lucky if you found a seat in the sanctuary, so the overflow rooms would be where I would normally sit. This particular Sunday when service was over, as I was leaving out with my daughter I looked over and it was the manager and lawyer Everett with his wife. When he saw me he lit up like a light at night and he let me know it was good to see me. Everett proceeded to tell me, "Marc

it's been over two years and I think about you every day."
He then informed that he thought about me because he
knew that I had what it took to make it big in the rap
game. He let me know that the meeting he took the twins
and Pops to in New York with Sony Music went well and
they let go of an opportunity. He let me know that he was
trying to get them a production deal, but Sony wasn't
interested in their beats, they wanted to sign me as an
artist. The vice president of Sony at the time David
Lawrence told them that if they wanted to make it, to get
behind me and push Marc Shyst and they would be big.
Well, the twins and Pops refused it and Everett told me
that he couldn't represent them any longer because of that
decision. It killed Everett inside to know that I had a deal
that was passed up for selfish reasons. He told me he
couldn't tell me because legally I was their artist and he
represented them. As he told me all of this in the church
overflow room, I was hurt, but I also was fulfilled. Fulfilled
because I knew my intuition was right about everything
and now I was given the truth. I got Everett's contact
information before we departed and he agreed to stay in
touch and to help me with anything he could and that was

a blessing to me.

*With knowing the truth of things about the twins
and seeing things clear around me, I stayed working and
moving forward. I kept pushing my mixtapes and kept
myself in the midst of the music business. A few months
later I got a phone call from Anton in California. As we
spoke he let me know that things with him and his brother
weren't working out and he was moving back home to
Maryland. This didn't surprise me at all due to the fact I
knew why they left now. I kept what I knew to myself and
never told Anton about it because at that time in my walk
with God I was exercising Gods heart of forgiveness. Even
though the decision they made left me without a record
deal, I forgave him in my heart and stayed in touch with
him. While fighting to keep myself going and working to
get a deal, I would always stay in touch with Bang Em,
Yukmouth, and C-Bo. Between the three of them, they
would motivate me with insight and they all gave me the
knowledge to the game through all the trials and
tribulations of life with music and as street niggas. Bang
Em was deported back to Trinidad for a shooting charge,
Yukmouth was forever getting involved with beef in Cali,*

and C-Bo had just gotten sent back to prison. All in all, I stayed focused and kept a level head. When Anton moved back to Maryland he would always reach out and call me and I would talk with him because I felt like he was trying to show his gratitude to me for what happened. He called me one day and told me he was back and trying to get himself back to music. He let me know he had set some equipment up in his house and was back to doing beats. He offered for me to come see him and I did. At the time I hadn't recorded in months and I was curious to see how he was doing. When I got there we greeted each other with smiles because it had been about three years since we last saw each other. When I got in his house, he led me upstairs to a small bedroom where he had a keyboard and computer set-up. From where their studio was when they left to where he was now was a total change. I could tell Anton was just glad to be away from his brother and wanted to get back to where he was when he left. We talked and laid out a plan to work with each other and mapped out The Pop Off 4 and called it 2000 Shyst year o the prophet because I hadn't recorded in a while and at this point, I had been through more than the average man could stand. I wanted to release what was in my heart with no features and so that is what I did. Everyone knew my spiritual side and how I blended it with my street music, so with this project, I set myself apart and brought it even stronger than before. Anton supplied me with some new beats and I killed everyone he gave me. In about two weeks I collected about twenty-five songs and had wrapped up The Pop Off 4, all recorded in a small bedroom with the impact of a big studio. I called The Pop Off 4 2000 Shyst, year of the prophet. In all, I was prophesizing my calling from God and displaying the talent he had blessed me with. After the music was done I reached out to one of my graphic designers and came up with an idea. I wanted the cover to represent who I was, an illustration of me at a table praying and, on the table, a stack of money, a gun, and my bible. So, I got with my man Mon 2 and sat down and we put it together. With new music and a creative CD cover it was ready to be released. What was created was a timeless classic body of work from Marc Shyst that captured the moment in time.

CHAPTER 13

CHOIR BOY

(Mark 10:27)

With man it is impossible; but not with God: For with God all things are possible.

By now I had my new mixtape done and history with dropping consistent music. My fan base and those who heard any of The Pop Off's were always eager and excited to hear a new Pop Off mixtape. What made my mixtapes solid was that I always gave up to date info on me, my life, and the things around me. I had been through so much at this time that I always had the raw material. So with my new mixtape and the space of life I was in, I kept pushing my mixtapes in all the mom and pop stores and in the streets. The thing that kept my ambition strong and kept me moving forward toward my goal of getting a deal was my faith. I had read the entire bible twice and when I finished the second time, I got a new King James version and began reading it for the third time. My bible kept me sane and kept my belief strong. It kept me strong in God and kept me faithful to my dream I had worked so hard for. No matter what, I never stopped working, but it seems trouble always would pop up.

By now I had a new project and I was back in the street pushing it. My friend named Tom that was with me the first time I got locked up was still hanging with me and seemed like he was really down for the movement. Tom would always say, "Man that night you got locked up, I was fucked up, I wish I would have taken the gun charge man." I knew he didn't really mean it and I would just tell him, "Nah you ok." I would ease his mind because even though he faked on me that night, Tom was loyal. He could beat the breaks off a gorilla for real, a real live brawler, he loved to fight and was built for it. One night I was headed downtown into the city to a club and Tom wanted to roll. So when I went to pick Tom up, he had his cousin with him. It wasn't that I didn't like Tom's cousin, it just wasn't my thing to do and I knew Tom was just showing off because he was always stunting to them about what he was doing with me, so I let him come. When we got downtown to where the club was I circled to find parking. As I pulled over to park, I noticed a tinted out car parked across the street. As I looked to observe it, the car speed off and pulled in front of my car, their front bumper to my front bumper. When the car pulled up it looked like some jack boys so I grabbed my gun under my seat. As I looked closer, the driver reached down and put a flashing police light on his dashboard. I quickly put my gun back and told everyone in the car, "Get out get out the car." When I said that we hopped out the car, and as we hopped out what proceeded out of the car in front us was four jump out cops, all in task force vest and regular clothes. When I got out I locked the doors and they pulled their weapons out and laid us all down on the ground in the street at gunpoint. When they whipped out their guns they yelled out, "Get down, get down, get down, right now." I could tell by how they were walking upon us, they wanted to shoot us while on the ground. While one of the officers was patting me down he went in my pockets and pulled out my car keys. When he got my keys I yelled out, "What the fuck you doing, you can't do that, my doors locked, I'm not even in my car." He proceeded to unlock my doors and search my car and he found the handgun. And here it was, after three months I'm right back in the same situation *again. With handcuffs on me in the middle of the street with Tom and facing another gun charge. I couldn't believe it, I was in all disgust with myself and I wasn't going to let Tom get off easy this time. The police had placed Tom, his cousin, and I in cuffs and set us on the curb as they kept searching the car. So I looked over at Tom and said, "Ayy Tom you got to take this one bra, I just got locked up three months ago for a gun and if I go back in they gonna fry me and I'm gone." Tom looked over at me and just dropped his head and didn't say anything. So I was like, "Oh you going like that, what happened to all that I should have taken the charge and I felt messed up bullshit." Tom just kept his head down with a frown and didn't say anything. So I had to remind him, "Look if something happens to me slim it's all over with, the dream, a deal, and everything." I told him if he took the charge because he wasn't a felon that they would just drop it and he would get off with just probation. I had just done it, so I knew. Tom looked at me again and just dropped his head and said nothing, as to say, "Nah I'm not doing it." I looked at Tom, shook my head at him and smiled with a smirk and said, "It's cool, I see you now cuz." At that moment I had a flashback of a dream I had two months*

ago. In my dream, a dog got close to me and bit me on my

hand. I remember asking my aunt Odessa at the time

what that meant. She looked at me and said, "Somebody

close to you as a friend will bite you," and here it was, all

that tough talk and this nigga froze up on me. What

followed after that was a total revealing scene from a

movie gone badly. The police talked with us all and I said I

didn't know anything about a gun, I heard Tom say the

same thing, but Tom's cousin had a long conversation with

the police. So they placed me and Tom in the back of one

cop car and then took his cousin in a separate car. I

thought that this was strange, but I knew it would come

out. The whole time in the back of the cop car Tom was

crying like we were facing life. I already knew this was

going to be a sixteen to twenty-four-hour process, so I

remained cool. I watched Tom break and fold as I looked

at him in silence. See I had been through the fire before

and now I could see that who I really was to him wasn't

who he portrayed it to be. Tom started crying out, "Man I

just want to see my kid's man." He was breaking and I

could see it clearly. When we got to the precinct to get

charged they placed me and Tom in holding cells next to each other, but took his cousin to a room around the corner where we couldn't see him. At this point, I could see that they were isolating his cousin because he was snitching. Tom's cousin was a good dude, not a go hard street nigga that did any time or was on the street hustling, and neither was Tom. Tom used to small bit hustle, but nothing serious, and this was his first time being locked up and he didn't want any parts of it. They began to bring us into the investigation room to get statements and charge us. They got Tom's cousin and walked him by our cells to the investigation room, once he was inside I started timing how long he was in there. This fool was in there for forty-five minutes giving info. I knew he was a rat at this point and that's why he was in isolation. They brought Tom's cousin out and when they walked him back by our cells he just hung his head low. Then they came and got Tom and took him in the investigation room. With Tom it was the same thing, I could hear his voice through the concrete walls, and I knew he was telling. I timed him and he was in there for about an hour talking to the police, too long not to give anything.

They brought Tom out and came and took me in. Once in the investigation room, they began to ask me questions and I let them know I was going to a club to perform and I don't know anything about a gun. They let me know everyone said it was mine, but I told them I needed to speak with my lawyer. I was in and out of the room in twenty minutes. I kept it straight and to the point, so they knew I wasn't cooperating with them. Once we left the precinct and they put us in the paddy wagon to go to the central cell to be booked and see the judge, I started putting my plan in order, so I could get myself out this mess. While being booked I prayed to God to lead my thoughts and words to speak. That morning when I saw my court-appointed lawyer, I laid it all out. I let him know they had searched me illegally, and that they went in my pocket, took my keys out and unlocked my door to search my car. After I spoke with him, they took me back to the bullpen and I waited to see the judge. It was now about four o'clock in the evening and we were the last to see the judge. When they brought me out and my lawyer stood next to me to argue my case, it worked. The judge dropped all charges due to an illegal search and let us all go free of no charge. When we were released I made up in my mind never to let Tom next to my glory and music again. If it were up to Tom, I would've been locked up, but glory to God that he saw fit to keep me free from jail and free from friends that will hang close because they want to reap the benefits of your success. After I made it out of the legal trouble with Tom again it made me reflect on my time and efforts that I was giving to make it. In reflecting I started spending more time in church and reading my bible. In doing so it lead me closer to God. I started attending a Tuesday night bible study at my church, which gave me a deeper insight into Gods word. One Tuesday night as I was leaving bible study an older man was in the hallway walking with his head down as in a confused state. As I approached him to exit the church, he lifted up his head and said, "Hey young brother do you sing?" I stopped and took a deep breath because I was getting ready to lie and say no, so I could avoid what he was saying, but I replied "Yes." I told him I was a hip hop artist and I rapped. The man then said he wanted me to come out and be part of the male choir. As he said that, I was thinking to myself, "Lord what have I done?" He then told me to come out that Friday to rehearsal and I agreed. As I left out the church I felt as if I had done something wrong and right at the same time. Wrong because I was a street rapper, but right because I joined the male choir. But after all the trouble I had been through I needed a new change of direction in my life. When Friday came around I prepared myself and left out to see what this choir thing was about. When I got to the church I went in and found the room upstairs where the rehearsal was. As I approached the room I could hear men singing and a piano playing. I stepped in the room, spoke to the choir director and took the closest seat in the bleachers. They then passed me a song sheet with the lyrics to the song we were singing. I started singing in my natural voice and going along with the choir. After about ten minutes of me singing the choir director looked over and asked one of the men singing, "Is he ok?" and he replied, "Yeah he good right here." I had taken a seat unknowingly in the bass section and that's where I was placed in the choir. The first night of me rehearsing was over and everyone welcomed me in. All of the men let me know I would do fine and I was met with joy and good energy. I remember leaving the church that night and with a feeling of goodness like it was going to be alright. What followed after that night was a few weeks of choir rehearsal every Friday night. During that time I learned a lot about life and what singing could do to encourage souls. One of the things that the male choir would pride ourselves on was that no one could really sing, and we definitely weren't professional singers, but we were all men willing to use our voices for God. The thing that made us great was that when we were all on one accord, we inspired the church and when we inspired the church we saved souls. That lesson was the greatest thing I learned. Not only was it the greatest, but the most important for me because I had made hundreds of songs, but now I truly understood how and why to make a song that matters. By now I was tuned in with the male choir and stood in my position in the bass section. Our first two performances were at our smaller church and we rocked the house, but now it was our time to sing at our new worship center. After our robes were back in we were ready for our big debut at the worship center. The day of our performance was a great experience. I loved how we would prepare the church for our pastor to preach and it

*made the church service complete. This particular week
we had a guest sitting in our crowd and it was BeBe
Winans, a popular and famous gospel singer. When the
pastor acknowledged him, he came up to the altar and
spoke to the church. BeBe then spontaneously sang a song
for the church. He turned around to the male choir and
asked if we could back him up and we cheerfully did. And
there it was, from me being a rapper from the streets to
singing with BeBe Winans. It was at that moment that I
became a true witness to Gods hands on my life. BeBe
sang and when he was done, the church was blessed and
he turned to us and blessed us. The male choir was the
transition I needed to grow. As I grew with the male choir,
I drifted away from rapping. I still had The Pop Off 4 and I
would still push my music to those that I wanted to, but I
stepped away from recording and doing shows. I never
stepped away with the intent of quitting rap, it was just
something that I needed time away from to release myself
of all the stress of not making it. After about a year with
the male choir, I was healed of a lot of things. I found a
new focus on my life and I was ready to get back into my
music. While in the male choir I still hustled my mixtapes*

to make money and build my fan base. That's all I knew how to do with my music and I never gave up, I just felt I had to find another way to get to where I was going. During my transition to finding my peace, I lost a lot of things and separated from a lot of people. I lost the relationships with people who held on just to see if I was going to make it big and felt I was done, but I kept moving forward and built myself up with a new way of life. A life that ultimately landed me in Baltimore City. I came to a critical point in my life and I made a decision to leave the male choir and leave Washington, D.C. Not to run away, but to gain more insight. With me moving to Baltimore I found a newness in my dream. I lived in Baltimore for five years and gained more insight into life. In Baltimore, I sold my CDs everywhere and I inspired the streets of Baltimore. To be honest, Baltimore supported my music and kept me alive. I sold hundreds of mixtapes and I built thousands of relationships with people and upcoming rappers. I learned a lot in Baltimore, I found my way and the streets gave me what I needed to be stronger. So after five years I returned back to D.C. and came with a new way to make it.

CHAPTER 14

VALLEY OF THE SHADOW OF DEATH

(Psalm 23:4)

Yea though I walk through the valley of the shadow of death, I will fear no evil, for you are with me; your rod and your staff, they comfort me.

Once I was back in D.C., I had another state of mind. I had learned more things while away, and the things I learned made me a wiser hustler and a better businessman. When I came home I could really see the lack in approach to the grind in the city, not only with hustling drugs, but also in hustling the music. By now in D.C., the music scene had changed, you had rappers like Wale and a few others who had major success with getting record deals. While a few rappers had record deals the radio stations in D.C. were more receptive to playing local artist to help keep their ratings. Rapping was still in my blood and it was what I had built a second nature to do, but I also knew financing your music was just as important as creating it. To finance myself at this point I was hustling and while hustling I stayed in touch with Anton and would go to his studio to record with him from time to time. While recording with Anton I was still somewhat lost, not lost in what I was doing, but lost in the direction that I would go with my music. I knew if I kept pushing forward that God would put me in a place to prosper. When recording with Anton from time to time I would sit and kick it with him about what he had going on and what I was doing in life. Things were a little different between us though because I just couldn't ever fully trust his direction anymore, I couldn't commit to just following him in the decisions of music. A part of me still wanted to help him one day see that I was the one that had the gift and calling to truly make it big for the both of us. The music we created together was great and creative and I believed in him to hold on to our friendship.

While back home there would be times I would go weeks without recording and I would be taking on my responsibilities of life. My Bible was still everything and I would always attempt to reach out to any resources I had that could help me get back on point and on track to getting a record deal. One day I was in Maryland in my daily travels and I stopped at a gas station to get gas. As I walked to go inside the store, a young man approached me and asked me, "Sir, do you have fifty cents?" My first reaction was, this little nigga too young to be begging for change, but I gave it to him because he asked. As I gave it to him he explained he needed to buy something out the store. I then inquired what he did to try to help this young boy out and give him some insight into life. He told me his name was Kel and he was a rapper and that he and his friends were on their way to an open mic. During our conversation, I let him know my name and that I was a well-known rapper in D.C. He really didn't know who I was, and I let him know that I would support his music when he dropped it. While we spoke at the gas station my mind started working and plotting on building myself back up to the point of getting back in the midst of what was going on in the streets as far as music. My thoughts to myself were that I would see what he was about and if he was good, I could put him under my wing and help him out. He told me that he recorded at a studio nearby and that he was working on his CD. We exchanged numbers and I continued about my night. Over the next few days, Kel and I talked over the phone and stayed in touch. Kel reminded me of myself when I was fresh in the game, just eager to record music and put out a CD. I would let Kel know about all my mixtapes and things I had done, and he would express how he just wanted to put together a CD and let people hear his music. Kel had a few other rappers he was in a group with and he wanted to introduce me to them and wanted me to hit the studio with them one day. As we stayed in touch, he let me know he had a few producers who were recording him and trying to help him get a record deal. I told him I would hit the studio with him to help him out with whatever they needed. See Kel was from the suburbs and was a lot different than my background. He and his little crew were all spoiled and their parents had money. Totally not the kind of guys I blended with, but I wasn't with them to hang and be buddy's, I truly gave them my time to help them and help myself. One day Kel and his group had a recording session with their producers and they wanted me to come and meet the people they were working with. My first thought was that I would go with them and see if the people they were working with were official and that there might be someone among them that I could connect with. The day of their session I met them at the studio where they recorded. Once I got there I came in and the first person they introduced me to was a producer by the name of Nardo. Nardo was an older street dude who at first when I met him was kicking it and more into checking Kel and his group on what they weren't doing right. Then they walked me into the recording room and introduced me to a guy named Troy when Troy met me, he shook my hand looked me in my eyes and said, "Marc Shyst right, you got some stuff on iTunes and YouTube." I thought to myself, he did his homework on me this might be who I came to meet. I sat quietly as they worked looking to see who and what else I would encounter. After a few hours passed and their session was over we left. When we left I was able to help Kel and his group a little better because I had more understanding of what they had, and what they had was a good opportunity. See the studio we went to was owned by Kel's grandfather, but ran by Troy and Nardo. Troy and Nardo were both producers who had worked with industry artists and they were helping Kel and his group put out a CD and eventually get them a record deal. Kel would always mention that Nardo had done a track for Biggie

Smalls and Troy had worked with a lot of people, but who Troy worked with he never knew. So I stayed in touch with Kel and his group as they needed me to give them advice and encouragement. Truly they wanted me to be a part of their group, but I was far too aggressive and advanced to be in their group. I would always let them know I was going to be there to help them, but I would let their group be their thing. Besides that, after all the groups and people I had helped and lead before, I didn't want to have that headache anymore. After going back to the studio with Kel a few times I noticed that Troy and Nardo would spend a lot to time trying to get Kel and the other members of his group to take what they were doing seriously. Kel and his group would fight with each other back and forth and do a lot of immature stuff that Troy and Nardo couldn't understand. Troy and Nardo would notice my maturity and wisdom with them, and they gravitated to me. Nardo and Troy were from the street, so we related on things that way and at times Kel and his spoiled suburb minded friends in his group just didn't get it. The thing Troy would do with Kel and his group took them out to the club and network, and they would invite me out with them. Troy knew a lot of people in D.C., and when we went out with him it was a celebration. The thing I liked about Troy as he was very humble, but connected to a lot of people. I was very observant to him as he was also to me, but in a silent way. Kel and his friends never really respected Troy though, they would overlook his kindness sometimes, but Troy never got angry with them he would just let them know they were playing too much. As things got hard for Kel where he lived, his family eventually kicked him out of their home for doing little dumb stuff around the house. So Troy let him move in with him at his apartment. Troy gave Kel a place to stay to help him out and try to keep him focused on his music. Kel's grandfather eventually closed the studio due to not having enough paying clients and not enough productive things going on. So Nardo went his way and Troy went his. While Kel was living with Troy I would go over to kick it with Kel when he would reach out and Troy would always be in his room on his computer or either on his phone. I used to think to myself, this guy is up to something. Not in a bad way, but I just had a feeling it was more to him than what Kel and his friends knew. Troy set up a little mic and computer to record Kel and his group while in the house. So after months of hanging around Kel and his group, they wanted me to get on a song with them. So one night I went out to Troy's apartment for a recording session. This was my first time working with Troy and I took it seriously because I knew he knew his stuff. Kel and his group were playing around as usual, but Troy was used to them by now. So Troy played a beat and I grabbed a pen and pad and in about twenty minutes, wrote a verse to the track. When I went in and recorded it Troy was like, "You did good Marc." I then went back in and dropped a hook for the song and called it, "Back In My Lane." When I came out of the booth from recording, Kel and his friends were being silly and joking like I didn't kill it, but I thought nothing of it and let them put their verses in. I left Troy's house that night thinking to myself, I know I killed that song, but no one was reacting to it, but left the thought alone. The next night Kel called me on my phone like, "Shyst, Troy wants us all to go out tonight, you down?" I agreed to go and they came and picked me up. Kel was in the passenger seat and his friend in the group drove while Troy was in the back seat. When I got in and we pulled off,

Troy said, "Man you killed that shit Marc, your verse was fire." Troy was excited about it like I had never seen. When I looked in the front, Kel and his group mate's faces were tighter than a little boy draws on a grown man. I could see they felt some type of way, and to the top it off Troy kept saying it over and over, "Marc you killed that shit." That night Troy didn't really have money like he always did so I brought him a drink at the club. Prior to this, Troy always brought Kel and his group everything, but no one ever did anything for Troy. So I did, and Troy saw my gratitude for him as a man and friend. That night Kel and his man in the group got angry with Troy in the club for not buying them a drink and they were at odds. Nothing new with them, but this time as we were leaving the club, their feud continued and while we were in the car waiting for Troy to get to the car, Kels friend says, "I'm bout to fuck Troy up." That's when I told him, "Nah slim you need to chill, don't even try that shit, Troy cool, yall just chill." Troy felt their vibe and ended up leaving the club with someone else.

The next day Troy called me and asked if I had time, could I come out to see him at his apartment, so I did.

When I got to Troy's apartment he was in his usual mode
of being on his computer in his emails and on his phone.
As we began to talk, he thanked me for buying him a drink
and began opening up to me. He let me know that he was
tired of always buying drinks for Kel and his partners all the
time and that it was nice for once someone did something
for him. I let him know that it was no problem because I
could see how he always looked out. Troy then began to
tell me how he liked what I did on that song I recorded
with them. He told me how Kel and his man would always
hate on me and talk down on me and say, "Man Marc
always talk about God and stuff in his raps." He said they
always tried to persuade him on not ever working with me,
but when I recorded that song he realized they were hating
and jealous. As we continued to talk Troy let me know he
would love to work with me and record songs to help push
me. He also told me that he and Nardo were working with
Kel and his group to get them a record deal because they
were connected to the music business. He was working
with them, but his efforts were being taken advantage of.
He told me Kel would go through his phone and steal
record exec's numbers to try to get deals without him, and

their constant immature playing and lack of respect was too much for him. Troy said he could tell I was different from them and a self-made man that knew how to hold his own, and that's what he liked about me. At the time I had a job at Bowie State University delivering packages and doing program setups while attending classes there. But the whole time I was a cold street hustler doing right to survive my dream. In the same manner, Troy was a lot like me. He had been through a lot of adversity and was doing right to survive the game, but deep down he was a cold hustler like me waiting on the right time to get back up.

Troy and I began to build a solid relationship together, Troy and I would still hang out and go to the club and I would take him around to appointments or wherever he needed to go. Troy eventually grew apart from hanging around Kel and his group as did I. It wasn't anything purposely done, it was just a new day of progress that Troy and I were moving in. Troy wanted to drop a project with me and was eagerly awaiting to do it, so he could get my music out. Not only were we plotting on music, but we were always strategizing to get back to the hustle and get our money up. Troy was getting a check every month and I

was still working, so we were good, if I had it he had it and
vice versa. Troy knew a lot of people in D.C., as did I, but
not like Troy. It amazed me how everywhere we went
somebody knew him and would call out, "Druppy," that
was his nickname back in the day. We never paid to get in
clubs and was welcomed everywhere we went. In the
same manner, he was amazed at the fact that everywhere
we went people knew me too. Sometimes the same people
he knew I knew also, that's when everything locked in with
us. He would always call me Nephew and I would call him
Unc, and that's what it was. I saw him as my gift from my
father, an older man that helped guide me and he saw me
the same, a young bull that would do anything to protect
him and was loyal. During that time, I remember one day
Unc asking me, "You know anything about lean," and I
looked at him and said, "Nah," because at the time I wasn't
too familiar and we moved on from it, but I could tell he
was thinking something that he wasn't telling me. After a
few months went by and we were hanging out and Unc
would slowly open up to me about things he never told Kel
and his group. He eventually told me how he was an A&R
at Def Jam Records with Russell Simmons and Chris Lightly.

Troy told me how he knew Puff Daddy, LL Cool J and a lot of other celebrities while working at Def Jam. Troy's biggest credits were producing a song for Biggie Smalls and he produced music on Heavy D's album as well. Then it all came together to me, Troy was truly the plug in D.C. He was tied to the hip hop industry like no other from D.C. He started the first record label in D.C., called Montana Records and he helped a lot of people in the city with promoting parties at clubs. All in all, he really believed in me as I believed in him. At the time I was still going to see Anton from time to time to record because I needed a studio to work at. I recorded a song with Anton one day called "Tryin See You," and when Troy heard the record he knew it was a hit and he loved it. When I told Troy who Anton was, he was familiar with him because Anton had done some business with Nardo and they sold one of his beats and ruffed him off with no credit for it. This was the type of thing that happens to producers that send tracks out to be used by other producers. Troy told me he got everything straight for Anton and got him his credit for a song he did and that was that. Troy used to tell me all the time in the club, "Nigga wait until we push your shit." He

knew we would be big in D.C. together, so we took the
record "Tryin See You," and we started pushing it in the
clubs. Since Troy was a promoter he knew all the other
promoters in D.C. that did all the parties in the city. So our
formula was simple, we would get the promoter the record
and he would make the DJ play it in the club. We used a
forced hand, and ultimately it worked. Unc had my record
spinning in the hottest clubs in D.C. every night of the
week. At the time the only artists from D.C. that was
moving was Wale, Fat Trel and Shy Glizzy had just come
out. They were hot, but none of them were in the clubs like
we were every night. So my fan base and popularity grew
and Unc loved it. Unc would always tell me how he was
going to reach out to Chris Lighty and get him to sign me
and I would get a deal, just that easy. He just wanted to
walk it out, meaning get my buzz up in the street and then
get me a deal. For a few months, Troy and I ran by
ourselves with very few people next to us, but as we
started buzzing, all his old friends and admirers would
come around to use him like they always did. Things were
different now though because I was with himand I
protected him and would knock the head off anyone who

got in our way. Unc introduced me to a lot of people and I introduced him to a lot of people I knew also. One person in particular that came around him was a guy named Trey. Trey was a schemer and scammer that always stole from Troy and used Troy all the time. When he came around, Troy would tell me all the fowl stuff he would do to him and had done in the past. But now when he came around I was in his way because I had Troy's best interest and kept my eye on him. Troy had his own history with Trey, so he kept him around to help with little things. Now that Troy was back moving in the club people from his past started to resurface. Trey was always envious and jealous of me because he couldn't steal from Troy while I was there , but he kept quiet about it because he knew I was Troy's muscle. I used to watch him every time he came around because I knew his M.O. He would lie and say Troy was his brother to people to get them to be lenient to him and go behind Troy's back to do business around Troy, a real snake type of dude. I use to ask Troy if he wanted me to dust him because I didn't like what he was doing to Troy, but Unc wanted to just let him be. Unc knew I would really hurt him because Unc knew how I went. People like Trey thought I was just around for something else and he feared me. He feared me because he wanted what I had with Unc, to be by Troy's side and he was mad because he was nothing like me. See when I was out with Troy I got all the pretty women, you know the models and top-notch strippers, I had them all because I had a natural glow and swag that attracted beautiful women. Trey would always come around with the little dirtbag hood rats that he had and we would laugh at him because being a snake that's what he did, crawl in low life dirt to plot on Unc. I would remember Unc's girlfriends would come back and tell me all the garbage Trey would say about me to them, and I let Troy know that I'm a hurt that boy. Trey would then come around us and act like we were cool. Me myself, I never had these issues, but it was one of those things that came with me and Troy making moves in the street. I never paid any attention to Trey because he was irrelevant to what Troy and I were doing, but it would be him and his backstabbing ways that would later resurface. See Unc told me how he would help Trey out by fronting his work and he would lie and say he got locked up and had to throw it. He would go behind Troy and try to sleep with his old girlfriends and lie about what he was to Troy to make it as if he was important. He was the worst person I saw around Troy, Unc made sure he kept him away from me because I never was for the games he played. As Troy and I moved forward things would become more intense with the jealous people around Troy, but as long as I was there, I kept nothing from getting in our way and Troy loved me for it. After a few months passed, Troy and I kept pushing my record and things were well. Troy eventually moved out of his apartment and moved into a house his sister Darlean let him live in. When Troy moved into the house I moved in with him. Troy set up his computer and microphone in a room and I begin recording a few songs. As I recorded a song or two Troy was impressed with what I was doing. He was excited because now I had made a few hits on his tracks that he produced and that meant a lot to him. With the new songs I had recorded, we continued to hit the clubs every night to push my records. I recorded a song called, "Bonnie and Clyde," and it was a smash record. I called a mutual friend of Troy and I's named Myah to do the hook and it was a classic. At the time Troy and I were making it out in the street and getting by with a few side hustles, but we needed more money to really make the moves to get my music out and eventually get me a record deal. After I had recorded seven songs my music was now starting to buzz and everyone who knew either me or Troy was aware of our bond of music and that we were shaking and moving. Troy had always been putting his hands in with lean and he had the resources to get it. One day Troy asked me to take him to see his old friend from back in the day named Bee. When we got to the hood to see Bee, he came and gave Troy eight hundred dollars and Troy left him with some more drink. I was amazed and in shock that this drink could bring in money like that. I was like, "Damn Unc this shit can bring in money like that?" Troy looked at me and said, "Yup" I told you Marc we was going to be alright. When we pulled off I told Unc I could help him move it because we needed the money to push my music in the street and he didn't have anyone else helping him. I put a plan together that night and the next day I got moving on it. After a few days, Troy and I started bringing in money together. Troy's friend Bee was a great help to us because he was the first person in D.C to help Troy move the lean in his hood. Bee and Troy *had a long history of hustling together. Unc told me he used to make sure Bee was good and Bee was buying keys of coke at fourteen years old. Well, Bee was thirty-five now and still getting money, Troy played my new music around Bee one day and Bee asked Troy what he needed to get me on. Troy told him he needed to get me a studio, and Bee did just that. He gave Troy the money he needed to get a building and put a studio in it. By the time everything was set up in the new studio business had picked up for Troy and I with selling lean. Troy and I were in the club every night, but now it was different, we weren't struggling, we were climbing on top and had a few dollars to play with now. At the end of the night when we left the clubs we would go back to the studio and stay there. I would record myself and Troy would go to sleep and when he woke up the next morning he would recite the rhymes I had recorded the night before. Even though he was in the back sleep, he still would be paying attention to what I was doing. I was expanding my clientele and so was Troy, it was good we were making money, but the people who it brought around would be the downfall of it all. See Unc was the plug, the lean he was selling he was* manufacturing it, in other words making it, which made us rich. I was his right hand, so I was the plug too, which meant you had to get through me to get to him in most cases. I knew he was manufacturing it and I never bothered to find out how, or what he was doing because we were a team and we made a lot of money. That wasn't the case for everybody else though who Troy brought close to him. People like, you guessed it, bum ass Trey. Unc would help out by letting him hustle for him and he was plotting to snake and steal from Troy. Troy was the type if you were bringing him money, he would serve you, he didn't care about feelings; he cared about getting more money. Besides Trey, Troy started bringing another one of his associates around named Playboy. Playboy was from uptown and was a real street nigga. Troy brought him in because he could move a lot of drink. The only thing about Playboy was that he used to try to size me up and figure me out, but never could. Playboy was never the jealous type of dude, he just wanted control of everything and couldn't put his hands on how to get to me. Troy tried to use Playboy as he did with me, to help keep people in the street off him if there was any trouble. I was a killer and so *was Playboy, there was a mutual respect, but I always watched everything because I knew that they all were trouble. As things got bigger we made a lot more money and created the opportunity we were waiting for. Troy got connected with an older hustler who knew some people of Yo Gotti and Troy did some promotion and business with them. When the dudes from Yo Gotti's label heard my music they were interested in me to the point of possibly working with me. Everything was right there for us then things started going left. I remember one morning as Troy and I woke up from a long night he was talking and mentioned how we were getting money and he wanted to just stack money to the ceiling. I told Troy that all the money we were making was good, but in my heart, I was an artist and doing music is what I wanted to do. With all that was going on and the distractions from outsiders, it was like our mission was now diverted. As things started to look up for us, it was one thing after another. Troy was signed to Chris Lighty and Russell Simmons along with Lyor Cohen as a producer. So Troy always told me, "When I get you to Chris you will be alright Marc." I used to ask him why we didn't just go to New York and take him the music.*

Troy would always respond with, "We alright, I want to walk it out and take our time." Well, one day out the blue Troy got a phone call and I was standing next to him, when he hung up the phone Troy looked up and said, "The devil always wins," and shook his head and said, "Chris Lighty just killed himself." I was hurt, but then I immediately fussed at Troy and told him, "Unc you got to stop saying shit like that." I understood his feeling of defeat, but I wasn't giving the devil that credit or recognition, my faith was too strong. It was frustrating to me because I knew if Troy would have listened to me, I would have gotten to Chris Lighty. I started seeing things go downhill and I kept the faith, but was watchful. I noticed how Troy was fading away from music and more interested in making money. I on the other hand I was ripping and running so much in the street, it was distracting me from recording. I would tell Unc, let's get my music out and drop my album. I was meeting women every night in the club and taking them out during the day, and by now I was a known player in the club and knew the game. It was all fun and games and Unc would be cracking up laughing at all the stories I would tell him, but I honestly was losing focus and was yearning for a stable life at the same time. I kind of started to see that Troy wasn't giving me the energy that was promised. So one day I was at my wits end and I went out to make a sale and had an altercation and I shot some people in a robbery attempt. I left the shooting and came straight to the studio, when I got there, I told Unc what happened and then I sat in the floor with my back against the wall in a zoned-out daze. I told Troy, "We got to put my music out or I'm not going to make it." I realized that I was risking my life and if I died I wanted to at least leave my mark with my music. Troy heard me, but it was like it fell on death ears because we never gave the energy to record. By now I could start to see what was more important to Troy and it wasn't the dream and the vision anymore, it was the money from selling what I helped him get off the ground. As days passed by I could see him gravitating to the same people that once did him wrong and now he was back hanging with them. He and Trey would go out and Troy wouldn't answer the phone when I called him. He would tell me how Trey would tell him not to fuck with me and my music and how he knew some other rappers that were better. I would tell Troy watch that nigga, but he and Trey were making moves together and Troy would tell me that's all it was. Every time Trey would come around, he would tuck his tail like a female and be like, "What's up bro," like he was cool with me, but I knew he feared me and to me, he was a coward too scared to show his face. Trey never knew the only reason I didn't break his jaw was because of Troy, so I played him off and let Troy have this fool around. Even Troy's man Playboy was showing his true heart. When Troy and I started selling him lean, he was down and out, but now he was making a little money and I could tell he was muscling Troy for control. Then one day Playboy came to the studio and was fussing at Troy about what he was doing selling with other niggas, so I stepped in and Playboy and I exchanged words back and forth. We hashed it out like men and that's when he started respecting me, or at least acting like he did. I knew he would try to make a move on me if I didn't move on him first. Over time we became cool, but I knew I had to watch him. Along with all the other B.S, this fool Trey brought his own set of niggas to the studio and they were all hanging out with Troy too. Dudes I didn't really fuck with, so I played them from a *distance and made my money with Troy, while he made*

money with all these other people too. I kept it cool, but I

could see clearly that Troy had changed up on me and now

he was headed in a whole different direction. All the

money we made together had changed him and he was

surrounded by bad energy, the energy that wanted me out

the picture for envious reasons and I kept my eye on all of

it.

CHAPTER 15

HEADED NOWHERE FAST

(2 Corinthians 4:15)

For all things are for your sakes, that the abundant grace might through the thanksgiving of many rebounds to the glory of God.

Things had gotten cloudy with the bond between Troy and I and at times it was frustrating. I had committed myself to make it with him and everything was in total chaos. When I saw there was a lack of ambition for music and no effort in making things happen, I had to reach out for advice from my old associates and business mentors such as Kenneth and Everett. Kenneth was a marketing and business genius that I met when Rico was working with me through Spontaneous Xstasy, a female entertainer managed by Tupac. Kenneth had gone through some things that brought him close with God and he changed his name to Asani Musa. Kenneth would always help me with things I needed guidance on. Both Everett and Kenneth gave me sound advice that I took to heart, but I was committed to seeing things win with Troy.

With all the new company that was brought in with Trey and Playboy, things were just different. There were times when things were stolen out the studio and Troy would look at everyone around like they had done it, the crazy thing was, I never had to steal anything from a man that I helped make money with. I knew it was the others around him and he just didn't see it. Everything came to an ultimate turn around one day when we were all supposed to go out one Friday night. I had a few runs to make and I told Troy and everyone at the studio that night I would be back in a few hours. As I was leaving Troy had placed a new bottle in my hand that had a full label on it, which was out of the norm from what we had been doing. With a room full of outsiders Troy mocked me and said, "Don't get caught with that now," when he said it I turned to him and said out loud, "I'm not going to stop." Everyone busted out laughing as if I were joking, but I was really being serious. I left the studio and headed around my neighborhood and made my rounds. As I was headed back to the studio I got a call from a close friend and fellow artist named KJ. KJ was my little man, a real street nigga, a real slash do whatever for the money type. KJ ran with me in the street and when he was down and needed anything I would make sure he was good, as he would do for me. When KJ called I was about to head back to the studio, and he said, "Hey Marc I'm fucked up and need to get to the store for some stuff for my daughter, can you slide through and get me?" I honestly had things to do, but I said yeah, I'm on my way. Now KJ lived in the heart of Simple City, a well-known housing project in D.C. Nothing out of the norm for me, but in the projects, there is so much criminal activity going on, that anything can happen at any time. I arrived at KJ's building and took him to the store down the street. KJ had been having trouble around his neighborhood at the time, being shot at and people trying him. So I kept a close eye on him all the time. As I pulled back in front of KJ's building to drop him off, I parked in front of his building and we said our peace and he got out my car. While I watched him walk in his building, I noticed he turned around and pulled his shirt up while watching him in confusion I looked over to my left side and saw a tinted SUV pulled next to my car. The SUV had crept up by my side and was so close that I couldn't open my car door to exit if I wanted to. While watching this truck, it crept by me so slow that it was obvious they were taunting me. Just then the back passenger window rolled down and a man with a hat on his head looked at me with a mean mug and frowned up at me. All I could imagine coming after that was a hand with a gun about to shoot. While observing the truck I could see that there were four people inside, so I was on alert that they might be jack boys or someone about to do a drive-by. The tinted truck slowly pulled up far enough for me to see that it had Florida tags and this made me think it was definitely a drive-by. Just then the back door of the truck opened and I slowly put my car in reverse and was easing back just in case they started shooting at me. As I was backing up I hear a "Boom" as though something was boxing me in. I then hit the gas hard and accelerated backward. When I stopped in the middle of the entry section from backing up, what I saw made me know it was a bad situation either way for me. I looked and it was another tinted SUV truck that I had bumped into trying to block me in. Just then all four doors of both trucks opened up with men hopping out on each side like a swat gang hollering at the top of their lounges, "Mother fucka, you mother fucka." Once I saw that I put my car in drive and pulled off like I was in the Indi 500 on the raceway. I remember thinking, "What the fuck was that, and now I'm on some other shit that fast." When I looked in the rearview, one of the trucks had begun to pursue me with a blinking light in their dashboard. My car came through the projects like a lightning bolt. I ran through a few stop signs and gambled with a high-speed jump over a busy Benning Road intersection. I made it out the projects and when I looked in my rearview again, they were still coming in hot pursuit of me. I then accelerated up to one hundred miles per hour on a busy street. As the cars came to a slow halt, I jumped into oncoming traffic to get away and sideswiped three cars until I spun out in the street at high speeds, which as you can imagine was extremely dangerous. My car, a black Chevy Impala, slid sideways so hard that I crashed my driver side door in the back of someone's parked car and flipped in the air. As I flipped in the air, it felt as if time froze and I was moving in slow motion. I knew I was in the air and I felt the car flipping. I opened my eyes to see me about to land in some trees with heavy branches poking out. I then said my peace with God anticipating that I was about to die from this impact and closed my eyes. Then I heard a loud crash and time jumped back to reality. I was upside down on the roof and hanging on locked in my seat belt. I released myself and fell out of the car into the street. When I got up it felt like I got hit with a sludge hammer on my whole left side. It truly felt like my arm was broken from the impact, so I took off running in the street. Just then I looked over and the police SUV was right there in 3D. The cop hit me so hard with his truck on my hip that I flipped in the street on my back. He then ran over my right leg and parked over top of me with his truck. The officer jumped out with his gun drawn on me with his hands shaking like a scared mouse in a cage. He scared me because I knew he wanted to shoot me, but he was too scared to do it. So I yelled out, "Ahhh I thought you were trying to rob me." I did that, so witnesses could look out their windows and it worked, crowds of people were now looking on. The officer then proceeded to kick me in my ribs while I was down and put me in cuffs. He was weak and his hits and kicks on me never hurt and I never resisted. He then, while I was cuffed, dragged me from my collar on my back scrapping my cuffed hands on the concrete so bad my hands were bleeding. What followed after that was total chaos. I then heard fire trucks, ambulances, police, and helicopters coming from everywhere. By now the second truck was pulling up and the rest of the jump out officers were there. One of them came running over to me and got in my face and screamed, "Look at all this bullshit you caused." At that moment I knew something they did was foul, and because of my injuries, the ambulance came and put me on a stretcher. While I was being put on the stretcher one of the jump out cops looked at me with a cold stare and mug like he wanted to kill me. He then yelled out, "You fucked, we found all that lean." I yelled out back to him from the stretcher, "You fucked when I sue your ass mother fucka." I was then placed in the ambulance with my neck in a brace and my whole body from my back to my legs hurting. I asked the ambulance people am alright in there and to make sure the police don't follow me. The ambulance let me know I was going to be ok and that I was secure with them. I was then taken to Howard University Hospital from the scene. Once at Howard they pulled me out and rushed me into an operating room with about three doctors and three students. They began checking me for injuries when they saw my pants opened at the knee and my knee bleeding, they cut my pants off with scissors to check me for additional injuries that may not have been seen originally. Once they finished checking me I was asked by the doctor how I felt. I let them know I was hurting from my back and hip where I was hit by the truck and that I was in a lot of pain. I was told by the doctor and police officer there that was on watch for me while cuffed to the bed, that if I wanted to stay at the hospital it would be all weekend until I saw the judge on Monday or I could get up and go to jail now and see the judge in the morning to be processed. I was in no condition to walk and I was in a doctor's gown at this point. So I agreed to be taken to jail that night and with everything in me, I limped out of the hospital bed to the custody of two white cops who were fueled with the same juice the first cops that chased me had. So in my doctor's gown, they placed me in a paddy wagon by myself to take me to the courthouse. Once in the back, they took off so fast that I slid back and forth and was in what I perceived to be unsafe driving conditions. I wasn't secured, so I was thrown around recklessly. They were both in the front *laughing and joking about it. They seemed to hit every bump hard and made every turn extremely fast. When I got to the courthouse jail I was brought in and taken to be processed. They fingerprinted me and placed me in a paper outfit, so I could see the judge in the morning. After a long night, they took me and about one hundred other people who had gotten locked up that night in D.C. in front of the judge. Once I saw the judge, I was released on my own recognizance to supervised probation and to get council. I left the courtroom banged up from the accident with a felony charge and in a paper jumpsuit for clothes. Completely embarrassed, I walked to the bus stop with my jail band and I caught the bus to the train station while on the bus people were looking at me in disbelief and fear like I was a monster. The reality was that I had been through a night of hell and this is what it looked like to survive it. Even the kids when they saw me were looking at me crazy. I then caught the train and made it home and back to the mess I was in. After resting for a few days, I immediately went to the studio with Troy and let him know my current predicament. I was now facing felony charges and a lot of jail time. I let Troy know I wanted to put my album out just* in case I went to jail and I had to do time. To me, that was all I could do to hold on to my dream. It was like it went in one ear and out the other with Troy. The months leading up my trial, Troy seemed to distance himself away from me, saying only, "You'll be alright" and then brush it off. It seemed to me it was no concern of his, instead of helping me with my music, he was hanging with all these outsiders wilding out and I couldn't understand how a person could change up on me like that. It frustrated me at times, but I knew I had to focus my thoughts on other aspects of my life. As my trial date got closer, the more I could see my end of things with Troy. Yo Gotti's uncle and his cousin who ran his label CMG would inquire about me to Troy and he would lack on following through with them. It all had me tied in a knot of disbelief, so I stopped worrying about recording my album and faced my destiny in court.

CHAPTER 16

ONLY GOD CAN JUDGE ME

(Luke 12: 11-12)

11. When you're brought before synagogues, rulers and authorities, do not worry about how you will defend yourselves or what you will say,

12. For the Holy Spirit will teach you at that time what you should say.

With my trial approaching, I wasn't scared, but unsure of what to expect. I had a court-appointed lawyer because with the charges I was facing, I was looking at twenty to thirty years in jail. I knew I had a case and my lawyer knew I had a chance to get off. The officers involved with my case wrote as many charges as they could to stack them against me. So I figured I would use a lawyer inside the courts to fight against them. My lawyer's name was Dan Harn, a middle-aged Jewish guy who was working his way up the ladder to his own practice. When I met with Dan he was very insightful about the process of my case. He let me know they offered me a plea of ten years. I refused it and then they came back with a plea of eight years and I refused that plea also. I let Dan know that I wanted to take my case to trial, so Mr. Harn very sternly let me know that if I lost at trial I would be facing a lot of time in jail. I had nothing to lose, so I put my faith in God and we filed for trial. A date for jury selection was given and we put together notes and a plan for trial. After a week or so the day of jury selection was upon us. In the courtroom sat the state's attorney and staff, the judge, and my lawyer along with myself. In the courtroom with us, there were seventy-six potential jurors that needed to be narrowed down to fourteen, twelve jurors and two stand-ins. Now, all seventy-six potential jurors were individually interviewed by both parties and the judge. The prosecutor selected those who would vote guilty in their favor, and we as the defense selected who we thought would give a verdict of not guilty in our favor. This was a tedious and very detailed process, but after about three hours of back and forth questions we had narrowed down the seventy-six potential jurors into fourteen jurors for my case. The judge then set a trial date for the following week and we were dismissed until then. The days leading up to trial were the worst because this was a serious case. If I

lost I would be going away for a long time and that was
the chance I had to take. My family and even Troy knew of
my trial, but everyone played me nonchalantly as if they
didn't have a concern about it. By this time it didn't
matter, I was ready to face my fate. As a court-appointed
lawyer Mr. Harn was doing his job to the fullest, he
brought on a private detective named Mrs. Shyrl who was
a jump out police officer in D.C. for twenty years. Mrs.
Shyrl knew her stuff and she was very key to my case
because of her knowledge and insight surrounding the
scenario of my arrest. Mrs. Shyrl filed for a copy of the call
into dispatch from the officers the night of the arrest and
low and behold the tape came back with the proof we
needed. The officers chase that night was illegal. Dispatch
never gave them the authority to pursue me, which is
against the rules of the D.C. police department. With this
as my defense, I felt like I had a chance to beat my case for
sure open and shut. It was the day of my trial, and a
Wednesday in the middle of the week. As we deliberated I
was nervous as a chicken in a fox hole. The judge, whose
name was Steve Nash must have looked over the case to
see what our defense was and made a false ruling. The

judge made a ruling and told my lawyer that the fact that the individual driving the SUV named Officer Pinto had pursued me illegally without dispatch permission could not be used in the case and deliberately told my lawyer not to bring up that fact during the trial. I knew then that I was in an unfair fight in court and that this judge was trying to ruin my chance of winning my case. When the judge said that I just shook my head in disbelief. My lawyer sat next to me and said, "It'll be alright we will find a way." The first thing I told my lawyer was that if I lose I was filing for the NAACP to look into this illegal ruling by the judge. Without any more delay the judge brought out the twelve jurors and the state brought out the arresting officers as their witnesses. The state took all day with calling on the three officers. We were dismissed from court to come back the next day. The next day, which was a Thursday, the state's attorney picked up with the same tactic of calling police officers to the stand. Well, his last witness was Officer Pinto, the arresting officer. After the state finished asking questions, my lawyer cross-examined the officer and set it off. My lawyer stood up in front of the courtroom and asked, "Officer Pinto, is it true that you were suspended by the department for the illegal chase of my client the night of his arrest." Officer Pinto agreed and said yes I was, just then the judge turned red and yelled, "I'm objecting to that question." "I'm going to ask the jurors to excuse that question and officer Pintos answers." The jury at this point was confused as to why, but they knew there was a cover-up. The judge then asked if the jury would take a dismissal break and they were escorted out the courtroom. When they left, the judge then looked at my lawyer and said, "Mr. Harn I cannot believe you asked that question after I strictly asked you not to." "I mean I am fiercely mad about this, I mean I can't believe this." "I need to take a break and think about how to deal with this." Judge Nash then stood up and took a fifteen-minute recess break, and walked out shaking his head while his face turned red.

When the judge left out, my lawyer grabbed his water bottle and said come on Marc follow me and we exited the courtroom to the lobby. As I was walking behind him I said, "Mr. Harn, you went hard as shit." He turned around with a scared look and said, "I know I could lose my bar for this." He filled his bottle with water and drank

from it like he had run a mile run. At that moment I knew
he was fighting for me and for him to risk his license, it
meant a lot to me and I knew he was serious. When we
gathered back from recess the jurors were brought back
out. It was my lawyer's time to finish cross-examination,
so he asked if they could play the dispatch call of the night
in question. When they played the tape in the courtroom,
you could tell that it had been tampered with from its
original version. Once the jury heard it, they were left
confused again because they were now privy to the fact
that the evidence was in fact tampered with. After cross-
examination, the judge stopped the court and released
everyone to come back tomorrow. The next day was
Friday and our last day of examination. It was now my
lawyers time to call witnesses to the stand. Our first
witness was, Mrs. Conoway, she was a resident at the
location where I crashed my car. She testified that there
were no sirens at the time she heard my crash, which
meant the cops lied about chasing me with sirens on. Our
second witness was Mr. Battle who's Cadillac I crashed
into, who also testified to hearing the crash, but no sirens.
My lawyer's last witness was KJ, who gave his testimony of

the night in question and me dropping him off at home, my reasoning for being where I was. It was the end of the trial and my lawyer thought I would have a better chance of winning if I didn't take the stand, but I wanted to. I wanted to give the court the true story of what happened. So I told my lawyer to let me get on the stand and ask me what happened on the night in question and let me tell my story.

As I got on the stand I leaned back in my chair and rocked back and forth as if I was at home and comfortable. I did that intentionally to let the jury see that I was comfortable and at ease about telling my side of the story. I gave my truth and recounted the events that took place that night, and at the end of my cross-examination, I shut the prosecution up. The state's attorney thought I would deny running, but I did just the opposite. I admitted running from the police in fear of my life because they were in unmarked vehicles. When it was all said and done, I got off the stand and left it in the hands of the courts. We took recess while the jurors deliberated and came up with a verdict. In about forty-five minutes they came back with a verdict and they called for me and my lawyer to come *back to the courtroom. My lawyer was nervous and so*

was I, this was my moment of judgment and I was facing a

lot of time. When the jury stood and gave their verdict for

felony fleeing and assault on a police officer I was found

not guilty. I was found guilty of reckless driving, which is a

misdemeanor charge. When they finished, the judge gave

me a week to come back for sentencing. As we left the

courtroom my lawyer and I celebrated with a handshake

and hug, we had done it. I stood up against the police and

the United States Government and won. While out in the

lobby of the court the jurors were exiting out and the jurors

that saw me came up to me and shook my hand and

congratulating me for winning. Even people that were in

the courtroom at the time were walking up to me

congratulating me on my win. I hugged my mother who

was there with me and left the courtroom. The following

Friday I went back to court before Judge Steve Nash for my

sentencing. After all, I had been through and beating the

severe charges, my lawyer and I felt that I would get

supervised probation and a few fines. That wasn't going to

be the case at all. For the mere simple charge of reckless

driving, the judge sentenced me to ninety days in jail and suspended all, but forty-five days. Then the judge looks over at me and says even though I was found not guilty, my actions do warrant me to do some jail time. In all disbelief, I was cuffed and taken to the back holding cell to be taken to D.C. jail to start serving my sentence. What follows is a diary log of my transition in jail called CONQUERING HELL.

10/4. As I got to the holding cell in the courtroom I felt faint. My lawyer came back to see me and apologized for this because we both knew that this was done to me as revenge for what Dan had done in court.

10/5. My first day in intake, my celli is cool, he's a real street nigga named Killa Cam. Cam is facing twelve to eighteen years for stabbing a man over thirty times. The average man would be in fear of him, but he was only twenty-four with a wise spirit. I enjoyed my time with him, he gave me a lot of insight about the jail because he was in and out of it.

10/7. My first day in population and the inmate in the cell they assigned me to came out with an attitude and we almost fought, they then moved me across the hall to another cell.

10/8. Got a bible from an inmate named Soup across from me, I intend to start reading.

10/10. Ran into Mike, a childhood friend of my little sister who remembered me rapping.

10/11. My celli Domo went home and it was cold in my cell. Today I cried tears of pain.

10/12. My new celli is from Sierra Leone and say 2 Pac is his father, Amen.

10/13. Had a dream I was in the studio with Lil Boosie and we made a song together called "All of my dawgs." I woke up and screamed out my cell "Free Lil Boosie." I got letters from my lady today and it uplifted me. Her love for me amazes me and keeps me hopeful for the future.

10/15. Today my celli from Sierra Leone's love for his kids overshadowed his faith and he lost it in the phone area. I gave some good insight into Abdul in the cell across from me about his case. Psalm 133 Unity. Fell asleep and had a dream I was in the biggest house I've seen, it was so beautiful. Just got a visit from my lawyer and he told me to write the judge for an early release. My lawyer asked if I would be a counselor because of my insight into the law and my character of understanding.

10/16. Today God saved my brother from Sierra Leone and

he went to a halfway house, we triumphed in prayer and gave thanks to the lord. When he left he hugged me so strong that he lifted me off the ground like a kid. Normally I would have been offended, but he cried tears and told me he didn't want to leave me and I told him he got to go home, so I can go home. I became used to being a blessing to people and giving myself to help them.

10/17. Got called out of my cell this morning for my first order of canteen. I was siced, as I got back to my cell I was going past my man Arvo's cell and told him I got him if he needed anything. As I went through my order I noticed I was missing the ten book of stamps that I had ordered. It defeated the purpose of ordering ten envelops to be mailed out. As I finished putting my stuff away Arvo came to my cell in a slightly down way. I asked was he good, he nodded like sort of. I asked what he needed and he replied just a little something. I told him I had seven noodles and what you need like two or something. He was like Nah just one will do. I tossed him a joint and told him if he ever needed more to holler at me. I stepped out in front of my cell and talked with him. His attitude was different today though. For the first time, he was in a down mood. He

- 271 -

stated he didn't have any money on his books to order canteen and to call his girl. He looked at me with this look like he was embarrassed slightly. He said "You know how you can tell when a nigga doesn't want to give you something?" As if he had asked someone else and they faked on him. I told him that "When you got it you got to help your people because the same people you see going up, be the same people you see coming down. I see it in the street all the time and niggas like that box themselves out from real niggas. He smiled and agreed, as he departed I told him to holler at me when he needed. After returning to my cell I continued to go through my canteen in disbelief about my stamps because this meant I couldn't mail out. I remembered then my partner David had stamps and was like ok, I know he got me. So I just situated my goods in a good position in my cell because now I had to guard my cell-like fort knocks from someone stealing. A few minutes went by and they called for top tier rec in ten minutes. When rec was starting the C/O was starting to let all cells prior to us out and looked in our cell and said: "That bed not made right." Shaking my head I was thinking to myself like that bitch. She then moved on to let the next cell out. I looked through our slot and told her to hold on I'm a fix it now, so she wouldn't leave us in. By this time she was at cell 57, I called her like "Hey C/O, she turned and looked and I told her I had done it. I asked her "What's your name?" because I didn't want to be disrespectful and call her Miss C/O. In a calm sarcastic way, she said just call me Serge. I smiled and said ok. She looked in and then yelled open 51. As she was there my celli started whining, "Man she just trying to be mean." I hurried and cut him off, like she good, just chill because I didn't want her to hear him and change her mind. My celli was young and his mouth had him say premature things at the wrong time. When we were let out Arvo was coming around the tier to pass by my cell, I stopped and we got to talking about music out of nowhere. I told him I heard him the other night mention that he was in a band. He told me that he played for the band TOB. It made me happy to hear this because I could see even clearer now that there was a possibility we could do something together once we were released. By now they were calling for lunch trays, so we took our convo to the line and got our trays together. We sat in the TV room and kicked it while we ate. He was directly across from me and me from him. He told me, "It's crazy that we could relate so much and we fellowshipped well seeing as though I was a Christian and he was a Muslim. He said that a lot of brothers in there run to it for protection, not for true brotherhood. I told him that God was good because we were both gifted individuals who could lead others. How we met, it was none other than the enemy trying to keep soldiers at odds with each other. He replied back with a nod and said I want to apologize for that too. At that moment I felt the power of God between us and scripture come to life. He could have brushed it off, but he apologized about it. I told him it was all right and it was nothing I took personal, I let him know I was in tune with our environment and I told him, "It's savage in this joint bra and its respect with us." He told me his mother had passed a few years back and some days it was hard for him, even now. We had the realist interaction at that point, I told him I needed him because I was a Christian and a believer, and as a Muslim, there was a lot he could show me to give me more understanding. He smiled and said, "When I was young my grandmother used to always make me read the scriptures before I ate. We talked for a little while longer and took our trays up. I told him we'd catch up later and we went our separate ways in the jail. After getting to my cell and working out for the evening, I washed up and prepared for the night. Just then my cell door opened, I popped my head out to see what was up and the C/O yelled, "Ball legal visit." I hurried and put my jumper on and went to get a pass, the strange thing was this time they sent me by myself. As he gave me the pass on a blue sheet I was in shock. They opened the block doors and let me out, as I was walking through the hall by myself I was thinking in my head, God has truly given me grace, because the place I feared going too, I had now conquered to the point of walking it by myself. As I came through the hall on the third floor I passed a holding cell with three inmates in it. I heard one of them yell, "Damn he walking the hall while count going on." As if to say, what kind of power he got? As I went downstairs to the second floor I passed another holding cell with about ten inmates in it. My man Big Chris was in it, and yelled out "Marc....what's up to Marc?" I yelled to him loud and with all the bass in my chest, I had, "Legal visit." I said it like that so that the other inmates in the cell with him would know I wasn't a game and serious. I continued walking until the guard stopped me at the legal room door. Once in I saw Mrs. Sheryl in there, she was on the other side behind a large glass. A female guard on the side where Mrs. Sheryl was, signaled for me to sit down where I was, and I saw Mrs. Sheryl walking around to come to me. Once she came in she sighed with relief and said, "These people are crazy, I've been waiting for two hours out here, and I said in disbelief, "To see me?" She said yes like it was ok though. I thanked her and told her it meant a lot that she came back. She then said, "I would have been here yesterday, but I was busy running around trying to get clothes for an inmate who went to trial yesterday." I told her it was ok because I knew if she could, she would come when she was free. I gave her my letter to the judge and asked if she could proofread it for me, to see if it was ok, or if I needed to make any changes to it. She then read through it and said, "Yeah....this should do it, its straight to the point." As I looked in her eyes I could tell she was tired because her blinks were slow as if she had to lift her eyelids with a crane. I told her I had thought a lot about what she and Mr. Harn said about me being a counselor and when I

got out, that hopefully, they could help me find a position.
We talked for a few, but as she stood to leave, I reached
out both my hands as if I was going to hold hands to pray
and held her hand and told her, "Thank you so much my
sister and I pray this goes through." As I said it, we both
smiled and she said, "Well hopefully when he reads it, he
will receive it in good hopes and let you out." I told her
again, thank you and hopefully, we would talk soon. As I
left the lawyer visiting room they moved me to the holding
cell on the second floor were my man Big Chris was
because they were still having count. The time was about
5:30 pm when they put me in the cell. I looked at everyone
nodded and said what's up, about six of them replied back
what's up, which was more than I expected to say
anything. As I walked to the corner of the cell where Big
Chris was, he said in a tired raspy voice, "Man Marc I been
in this joint since three o'clock. I told him in a shocking
voice, "Damn holmes, my private investigator been up here
for two hours waiting to see me." Big Chris was like, "Man
they fucked up in here moe." As we talked for a little while
longer a few more inmates in the holding cell while they
were finishing the count. Ten minutes went by and an

inmate came from downstairs walking in shackles on his feet and cuffs. One of the dudes in the cell with us yelled out, "What's up Dee, you just getting out the hole?" He smiled in a crazy way and was like, "Yea." The inmate in the cell with me asked him "Where Rell at, he still down there?" He said yeah he there as the C/O walked him by. Right then another inmate came from downstairs in shackles to go back to his unit. One of the inmates in the holding cell yelled out, "Ron what's up Ron, how yall make out?" Ron smiled in happiness and yelled out to the dudes, "We lost cuz, we lost all sixteen counts." With a smile on his face in a happy mood, he said, "I'm all right though," and went to his unit. I saw the seriousness of time given to our people in jail and it's a lot of our harsh realities. They held us for about twenty more minutes and let us all out after count to go to our unit for the night.

10/18. I woke up to the loudmouth younging making noise talking loud to the inmate in cell 52 next to me.

10/22. Woke up early this morning to a dream of being inside Club Ibiza in D.C., I was performing with Bone Thugs in Harmony and Tupac came out on stage, happy to be in

D.C and ripped it. I then woke with a flashlight in my face from a C/O checking count. It made me so mad I woke up in anger and went back to sleep. I then dreamed I was in a room with Jay Z and his daughter Blue. Blue liked me and wanted to be around me and Jay was looking surprised at her. It was like she liked my music or something.

Finished the fourth chapter of my book, "The Tupac Code," I'm so motivated right now.

10/23. Today I finished reading the book of Ecclesiastes, it has given me more strength to my spirit. I went under attack with my daughter's mother heavy today. I conquered my thoughts with prayer. I wrote a letter to my mother today to let her know her son was good. Started working on chapter five of, "The Tupac Code."

10/24. Today I read the book, The Songs of Solomon, now I'm doing my notes from Ecclesiastes to hold on to what the Lord has shared with me. My daughter's mom has been heavy on me today too. There's a part of me that the devil knows he can get to me through her. I pray she is well and I'm conquering my thoughts with God's word. They moved a few new youngins in cells next to me today.

They came from the hole and they were rowdy, I know they're plotting on stealing from niggas.

10/25. Started reading the book of Isaiah and woke up with prayer. I kind of got into it with my cellmate next door while fussing about block detail. Things are cool though, I had to just control myself, something I'm working on. The correctional officer Ms. Wisely has been bringing me my letters the last few days and today she sort of flirted with me. I have my daily routine of writing my book, working out and reading.

10/26. Tried to go to bible study today but the C/O wouldn't open my cell. For the first time, I kicked on my door, "Boom Boom Boom Boom..... until she came. She was a C/O I had never seen working before, she denied me to go to bible study and said we would go out tomorrow for service. When she denied me, I felt empowered because no man alive can keep me away from God. I finished chapter five of "The Tupac Code" today and I'm progressing.

10/27. Went to church service today and prayed. I received the word that the pastor gave about Jesus. The youngins in my section got rowdy today, I witnessed a young man from Maryland fake as though he was from South East until little loud mouth dude called him out. D.C jail brings the real out or exposes the weak.

10/28. Had a dream last night that I met 50cent and Floyd Mayweather. In the dream, I took a picture with both of them and 50cent told me he was excited to work with me. I asked him how I could get in touch with him and he said call me direct and gave me his number. Today we had our own bible study in our section at about nine o'clock. We started with three people and then my man David came and joined and asked will we be doing this every day. It was what I knew God sent me here to do. The youngins acting rowdy from last night quarreled with each other. I stopped Abdul from fighting while we were getting haircuts, he later thanked me and told me to pray for him.

10/29. Had a few dreams today, and then I was awakened by a visit from discharge that notified me of my release date and medical benefits I could get once I'm released. I had a dream today that my daughter's mother had bought me about ten watches, all fly. I had another dream that

Wale was up at the jail using the jail for a video shoot and it angered me because I felt he was showing them my lifestyle, essentially a place I survived. My cellmate is going home on Thursday and I can't wait. His immature outburst and lack of understanding of a man's situation frustrates me at times, but I give him all the teaching I can. He is an obvious mother's boy who talks only about sex. Yesterday I had to give him advice a man would give his son on having babies. I actually teared up tonight thinking of the bible study yesterday and how with God I have conquered and seen him move in this hell.

10/30. Woke up this morning to the disrespect of my next-door celli dropping his breakfast tray in front of my room. I had to bass on him and let him know I wasn't going for it. We had words back and forth and I knew it was tension. When they popped our cells he came to me with his hand out, and I shook and agreed to him that I only wanted to help him know what right from wrong in here. My work out today was well, I can notice everyone watching me either in envy or jealousy. Brothers now approach me as I work out and say they gone start working out with me (yeah right). Today was crazy as all the youngins still argued out their cells to the point of aggressive words. As I worked out a few came and consulted with me. My young celli go home in the morning, his constant talk of it drives me crazy, and he's too young to know to just shut up. I will be glad when he's back home, jail is no place for him. I had an evening nap and woke up to one of the detail men staring in my cell, it made me furious. It took all of God's love and mercy to let it go.

10/31. Woke up this morning to get canteen, and the Mexican man who is in the cell across from me gave me a bag of chips and a soup. He prays all the time and he knows I'm on God's time. Sometimes you receive, so someone can receive their blessing. The young man who was in cell 52 next to me today finally had his foolishness catch up with him. He acted out of character for about a week until tonight his fear allowed him to check into PC. This place will call out your weakness.

11/1. Early this morning after breakfast trays my cell popped open for pill call. I went to see if it was my flex all for my back pain. The nurse said he had something for me this one time only. When I took the pill it knocked me out *fast asleep. Afterwards, I wished I hadn't taken it. I now know there are some things once released I won't be doing. Two inmates I know got into a fight tonight as I worked out. They were both Muslims and I had a bad feeling about it, so I prayed to myself for them. Twann and I went back to our bible study today and had a spiritual talk, sort of like the second bible study. At the end of the night my brother Twann came back to talk more Bible with me. While I was in my cell talking, another fight broke out with my old partner named Silk and the guy he was fighting pulled out a knife to stab him. Jail is a dangerous place and the actions you do in here add up to trouble quick if you're not strategic. Finished chapter six in my book today.*

11/2. 4:00 am- As I read Isaiah 42, God promised me a new day of delivery for me. I received his word of my promises to a people of prison. I shall go forth and make darkness light before them. As I read I understand why I am in the prison house.

4:25 am- Isaiah 43 Declares his will for me and what he shall bring forth. I will hold God to the words of this book, as he has directed me to. Today they paired everyone in cells, so I got a new cellmate. He seems to be cool, but only time will tell. I've been in my cell since Thursday by myself and kind of got use to the peace of mind. At this point, I can make it with anyone who got a mustard seed of sense. Today I had the biggest headache, I think from everything that took place yesterday. Tonight I'm a workout and try to take it one day at a time.

11/3. Today was an alright day for the first time since I've been here. I came out to watch the Redskins game with the whole jail. When they called for church service I decided not to go in order to call my mother. When I reached her, she told me she had prayed in church for me to call her today. Afterwards I called my baby to surprise her also. When the church was over there were a few brothers that noticed I wasn't there, and they asked was I ok. That was a good feeling to be looked at as a man of God. There was another fight in my section today, so I checked on them both, Kumar and Love. I pray for my people. The issue with my new celli's odor was resolved like men. Amen to the lord.

11/4. Today I rested in my cell like I never have since I been in here. I've never slept that much, a part of me wanted the day to just go by quickly, so it could be over with. I got a letter from my daughter's mother today that uplifted me. My new celli was telling me some stories today that had me cracking up laughing. I never laughed that hard since I've been in here.

11/5. Today my brother Twann and I sat down and had bible study again. When I walked up he told me just the man I wanted to see. I can tell he really is intrigued by me as much as I am with him. I told him I know he is a true believer that can build with the body of Christ outside of jail. My celli and inmates have had me laughing with tears for the last few nights. I can tell my surroundings have a respect for me that I can appreciate. Today my mother sent me a letter and it meant the world to me. My celli next to me in cell 50 is a cold thief and wild youngin. I knew this about him and I gave to him when he asked and yesterday my cousin came to me and told me that the wild youngin told him he fuck with me hard. It meant a lot because I saw he does respect me. Then my brother Twann shared a scripture in Luke that gave me insight on it.

11/6. Finished chapter six of "The Tupac Code" and started chapter seven. Had another inmate who came in my unit yesterday check out today. He came in asking a lot of questions and I knew he was in fear. He said he was from Simple City and I could tell the environment was too savage for him. I heard him when he called the C/O over and checked out to PC.

11/7. Finished reading the book of Isaiah this morning. Wrote my little sister a happy birthday letter today and mailed it off, so she could get it by Saturday. My day was spent resting and fellowshipping in my unit. I had a Bible study tonight with my man Twann. He went to court today for sentencing and received 18 months, suspended all but 6, Amen. He received a blessing that I saw God do for him. I watched the Redskin game today and then rested in the fact that I only had three more days until I got released.

11/8. Got awaken by the C/O telling me I'm getting released today! I was scheduled to get released on Monday, but since it was a holiday I got released three days earlier, Amen God is good and now is my time and my season.

CHAPTER 17

POSSIBILITIES

(1 Peter 5:10)

And the God of all grace, who called you to his eternal glory in Christ, after you have suffered a little while, will himself restore you and make you strong, firm and steadfast.

When I came home from jail I had a new perspective on life. I was stronger than ever in mind, body, and soul. I had left a few thousand with my people until I got home, but after paying a few bills and a few other things, I came home to eight hundred dollars, which to me was good because I wasn't broke. I knew my clientele didn't know where I was so the first thing I did was pay my phone bill and I was back to business. My phone rang in less than ten minutes of me turning it on. One of the first people I spoke to was KJ who let me know he couldn't find me and reached out to Troy and spent some money with him. I let him know it was all good, but I wanted to see if Troy would let me know or cut me out of the money KJ spent with him. After that, I visited my mom's house, then went to my daughter's mother's house and just soaked up being back home and getting back to life. The next day I called was Troy to let him know where I had been. When I spoke to him he let me know that he was worried about me and was checking around to see if I was locked up, but didn't check D.C. jail. He also told me that he had got a call from one of my customers and he had some money for me too, which was a relief because I needed to get back up on my feet. After we spoke for a few minutes he said, "Well Marc, I got to tell you this because you got to know." He took a deep breath and said, "I got to have surgery to take cancer off my lungs and another to remove a tumor off my brain." I was in shock and disbelief about what he just told me. I told Troy everything would be ok and that I would be there with him to see him through it all. The next day I went to see Troy at the studio and he was a little down, but he was happy to see me. I gave him details on where I was and what happened in court. That night we went out to the club and all of the people around Troy were people that weren't good for him, like Trey and one of his older buddies named Sam. Sam was an old nigga that was always trying to hang around and chase women. He did this so he could find out who your women and he could down talk another nigga to get sex from the girl. Something he did with Troy, but I would always watch him because I knew he was a snake. Sam was always out looking for niggas to rob in the club, Troy never really trusted him and would tell me sometimes, "If something happens to me I'm with Sam. When that night was over, I met Troy back at the studio and we talked about how we were going to move forward with everything. We sat up all that night and had a real heart to heart. Now that Unc was sick he wanted to take my records that we had, mix them and get my CD together before he had surgery. I was glad to hear him finally say he was going to get to my album, but the reality was that he was very sick and with two surgeries coming up, he was giving me his last push of energy to give me my just due. He also let me know what was going on around him as far as business. While I was in jail Troy started hanging with Trey and Playboy even more than before and a lot of bad things went down because of it, just as I knew it would. Troy told me how they both got close enough to him to find out how he was making the lean and they both stole what it was they wanted from him and cut him out of making money together. Trey went as far as stealing Troy's clientele and never looking back, Troy was furious about it, but acted as if it didn't bother him. As for me, I saw it coming from Trey when it came to Troy a mile away, it's what he always had done before and I warned Troy about letting him in, but he did what he wanted and got betrayed by him again. Outside of that, Trey was going around trying to do parties and go-go shows with Troy's people that he met through Troy behind his back. Trey would use the "My brother Troy" line to get sympathy, but Troy was not his real brother. Trey was a real snake type of dude with no substance to stand on so he always took from Troy. Troy let me know that he and Playboy were on the outs about some money and business they had done together. Their situation was serious though, it was bad enough that Playboy wanted to kill Troy and Troy was going to get him killed if they bumped into each other. Outside of that, Playboy learned how to make lean from Troy and went his own way and cut Troy out. I always looked at the situation with Troy and them as bad energy and karma catching up to Troy for changing up on me and bringing them into what we had going on. Even after all that was done, I still stayed loyal to Troy because I knew God put me in his path for a reason and I wasn't going to leave him with no one there for him. Following that we stayed in the studio putting all my songs in order and getting my CD done before he had surgery. After we finished my album we had a classic project. The songs were so good that I put together, that I called the project, "2 Good 2 Be A Mixtape." When the album was finished Troy was looking for one of his industry connections to help push my album and get things going. He reached out to his partner Greg Baker and he put together a plan with Greg to get me going and moving in radio and promotions. Troy paid Greg two thousand dollars to get started on my promotion. After that Greg was a no show, he basically took Troy's money and never did the work he had agreed to. Troy wanted to sue Greg, but I told him not to do it. Greg was a good dude and I don't know why he didn't hold to his obligation. I knew that a lawsuit would cross the lines of everything, so I told him not to do it. So Troy told me he had another guy that worked in the music business and he could do the same thing as Greg. Troy set up a meeting with his man named Dre to come to the studio to sit down with us. Troy told me, "All we need for him is to like your music and we're good." The day of the meeting was upon us and our meeting was very successful. After talking for a few minutes we played some of my new records and Dre was on it. He liked what he heard and wanted to work with us. As we talked more Dre let me know that he used to work for Violator with Chris Lighty. Dre used to do street teamwork in New York with all the rappers and he knew the business. Dre also knew Mike Lighty and Dave Lighty, the brothers of Chris. I knew Dre could help us and he did. As we start setting up a plan of things to do to push my project we were all inspired at first, but after a few weeks Dre could start to see the things I was seeing in Troy. It was like he lacked ambition and he became a negative voice of perception on our team. So Dre and I would stay motivated by pushing my music how we could. Dre couldn't understand why Troy wouldn't use his connections in the industry and get them my music. Dre knew Mike Lighty very well and Mike was a very well established booking agent in the rap game. Dre decided to do what he could to help me without Troy knowing and sent my music to Mike Lighty. Mike loved it and had a plan to release my music so I could start a buzz and get known in the game. When we told Troy he was nonchalant and acted as if he didn't care, which threw Dre and I off. We couldn't understand why Troy was so negative, but we never let it bother us. Things with Troy's procrastination and negativity got worse to the point of aggravating Dre and he stepped off from doing business with Troy. Dre would stay in touch with me and always check up on Troy to make sure he was ok. By this time Troy was going into the hospital for his first surgery. Unc made it through his first surgery successfully, the doctors managed to remove the cancer from his lungs and patched him back up. I was there to see him through it all and it wasn't easy for him at first, but he made it back home and on his feet. While he was recovering I was still working recording new songs and staying in touch with the people that helped me with music. While Troy was healing up, his troubles would never leave him. Trey was still coming around here and there and things with him and Playboy were getting worse to the point of them beefing. All and all with him healing up, Troy still had another surgery to the face, the doctors still had to remove the tumor off his brain. So three months after his lung surgery he went back to the hospital to have his tumor removed.

When Troy went back in for surgery this time it was hard on him. After the surgery was completed there would be times when he would sit there and cry out in frustration. I would always encourage him to know that he was going to make it back on his feet and we were going to get back to our plan of getting me a deal and getting out the streets. When Troy came back home from brain surgery he still stayed at the studio and I stayed at the studio with him to get him back and forth to his chemo appointments and making sure he was eating right. Troy's fight with cancer came back when he was recovering and he died about six months after getting out of the hospital. My heart was torn and when he died a piece of me died too. I never saw this coming and I couldn't believe my uncle, my mentor, and partner was dead and gone. I knew he was a special man while I was with him, but I never would have thought that what we did together was for me to learn and walk on with it, and give it to someone else. For the six loyal years that I spent with Troy, they were the best years of my life, I learned so much in such a short time. I spoke at his funeral and gave my insight about him. At his funeral I was his protégé, I was the one he gave the jewels to freely. I knew the truth of his livelihood. Days before he died Trey wanted to see him and Troy told me don't let him, he told me to tell Trey to just give him his money. I remembered that because at his funeral, this fool came in late and disrespected his funeral coming in smelling like weed. I knew he couldn't face Troy's death sober, so he had to smoke to cloud his fucked up thoughts. I wanted to break his neck, but I knew Unc would tell me don't do it Marc, so I kept it cool. We had Troy's funeral and I kept his vision alive. The vision of what we had set out to do with each other when we first met.

Days after Troy's death I had to snap out of my depression and thoughts and I did just that. I started working on new music to release because the album me and Troy did never got released officially. I wanted to put it out and I did. I just released it online as a free download to let the music get heard. After that I immediately started working on new material with Anton. Anton had my back through the whole process of me losing Troy and our bond became stronger as men. While working and recording with Anton I began networking with all my new producers and dropping songs that had a new and updated sound no one had ever heard from me. While recording I was still ripping and running hustling even harder than ever to finance my dream. I was going to the club every night like Troy was with me and still networking with all the people we would kick it with together. All in good spirits of his life. Dre and I still hung tight with each other, Dre plugged me in with Mike Lighty even stronger. Mike Lighty and Dre set up a plan to release my new music as I got closer to finishing my songs. Since Dre got me to Mike Lighty, our relationship became stronger. Mike was the booking agent for Rick Ross, Cash Money, and a lot of mainstream hip hop artists. Mike was working with Yo Gotti also as his road manager, so he always gave me good insight on what I could do next. Things were coming together for me, so with the help of Anton and a few other producers, I started a company named Orchestr8ed Hitz. The company was a production/record label that helped make hit songs with great artists. Sort of the same way that Troy did with me. With a new team of producers and a few artists that I was producing, I was ready to release my new CD titled "Pay

Day." Mike Lighty put together a plan for me to have Waka Flocka's DJ at the time named Big Tiny to host my tape and get it out to the industry. While waiting for things to line up for the release of my new project, I was introduced to a booking agent out of Atlanta that liked my music and wanted to help me do shows on the road and build my brand. The booking agent wanted to get me traveling and that's what he did. I signed an agreement with the booking agent and was on the road doing shows from New York to Atlanta. As things were happening, I could notice how things were falling apart too. The project I was set to release with Mike never launched due to the DJ and Mike not following through with our agreement. I was seeing the gaps of truth from my booking agent also as I continued to do shows with him. I wasn't getting paid what I was supposed to be getting and I had to stay on top of my business stronger than ever before. Outside of that at home in the DMV, all the bad energy that was around Troy while he was living was now prowling around me. I ran into Trey out and about and saw him clearly. After Troy died he went to all the clubs that Troy worked with and used that Troy my brother line to get in to promote.

He had found some light with promoting because now that Troy was dead he could snake Troy even more. When I saw him he made the statement of, "Yeah now that Troy dead I'm like running things now." I looked at him as a joke because I knew his whole scheme flat out. I felt that if stealing another man's identity when he died made you feel like a man than let your soul have what it desires. I kept it humble with him, but I could see the hate and envy in him because at the same time he never helped me with what he knew I was doing and made sure he tried to box me out. Sometime later Trey's immature fraudulent ways caught up and someone shot him like ten times outside his house over some stuff about a girl, but he survived the attack. I would always say that Troy tried to help him, but he just loved to steal from him. When I saw Playboy he was on the same bullshit. Playboy had made a lot of money in the streets selling the lean Troy showed him how to make and he still would act like Troy was his enemy. Playboy had changed and all the money did it, he was acting like he was all that and a boss, but I remember when he was fucked up and we gave him a way to get it. I could see it in Playboy too, that I couldn't trust him, so I played him from a distance to let destiny give everyone their fair share of light. Then there was Sam, this old ass fool came around me trying to hang out like he was cool with me, but the whole time plotting on me like I didn't know what he was doing. I eventually called him out and he never came back around. I told him I was going to fuck him up for some back door shit he tried to pull on me with a girl. When I look back at it all I was being attacked by the same energy that Troy was dealing with except for me, I wasn't Troy and I was time enough for it all. Things took a turn for the worst for me a few years after Troy died. I was pulled over in Maryland and racially profiled for the type of car I was driving. At the time because of all the crazy stuff going on in my life, I was on high alert and on the lookout for trouble and it all caught up. I was driving in my Audi and when the cop pulled me over I had a loaded gun in my car. The police did me dirty though. They never asked for license and registration when they pulled me over, they surrounded me with eight officers with guns drawn, dragged me out my car and cuffed me. When I asked them what I was being pulled over for they told me to shut the fuck up and acted as if I were a robbery suspect. They searched my car and found a loaded gun. The police acted as if they found Sadam Husain and threatened to shoot me about five times. They took me to the station and brought in homicide and interrogated me for nine hours about murders and shootings. They went as far as writing up a fake statement on me. When I got to the commissioner they set my bond for $400,000 and charged me with fourteen felony counts. So I sat in jail for three days awaiting a bond hearing to get a reduction and they dropped it down to a $20,000 bond. When I got out on bond it was like everything went downhill for me. I stopped moving in the streets because I knew the police were monitoring me, so I moved out of my penthouse apartment, sold my cars and changed my direction in order to make it through this part of my life. I lost everything and everyone around me. My booking agent backed up from me, I had my mentor and friend Everett back up from me with a campaign we had set up. Everyone thought that life was over for me. To be honest it was a part of me that died and I let it. I let everything around me go and I started rebuilding a new me. With the help of my good friend and agent Asani, I started a company promoting parties to learn the ropes and gain leverage with my music. I began acting in movies and I started my own painting company. I was still recording from time to time, but beating this case was the most important thing in front of me. Things started turning around for me as my new case went forward. They charged me wrongfully, so fourteen felony charges got dropped to four felonies, and then from four felonies to one misdemeanor charge. The state's attorney was embarrassed so much that the police raided my mother's house to see if they would find more guns or drugs were I stayed. I wasn't home at the time, so they approached my mother. The police planted a box of bullets in the house and asked my mother to sign a paper saying that it was mine. When she denied them and said no, they left and the police never mentioned it again. During all that, I kept working hard promoting and hosting parties. My promotion company got me close to the industry and sharper with my business. I was asked to host an industry night in D.C. with a few record labels looking for talent and I killed it. That night I met a guy with a distribution company and we talked and got familiar with each other. Two months later we met and had a meeting. After the meeting, they signed me and gave my company a global distribution deal for my music. This was big for me, not only did I have my own label, but now my label had distribution.

At the same time, my court date was getting closer and my lawyer had only a few options. He told me with a case like this that I was more than likely going to have to serve jail time. He told me I could fight the case and face up to five years if convicted or take the plea the judge was giving me and hope for the lesser of the sentence. As much as I knew I had a case of wrongful doing with corrupt police, it was my word against theirs and I knew that the police had falsely put things in my case to get me convicted. So I took the plea, and signed my life away to a misdemeanor charge and faced up to two years in jail. When my lawyer handed me the plea to sign in court, I was shaking like I was outside in freezing temperatures. I felt God telling me to trust him and I did. The judge took the plea and gave me a month to come back for sentencing. My lawyer told me that was a good sign because she could have locked me up then if she wanted to. When I came back for sentencing, I had letters from the movie director I was working with in Philadelphia, letters from my booking agent and letters from my mentor. The judge took into consideration my acting and music career and gave me thirty days in jail with a year of supervised probation. When the judge gave me my sentence I was relieved. My first thought was that thirty days in jail is what I needed after the stress I went through. When they processed me and put me in the processing unit, I was placed in a cell with a Korean man named Bill, Bill was cool. As I got situated in my cell Bill sat in the top bunk reading his bible. While looking around my cell I noticed bloodstains on the walls and ground. Bill let me know that a Mexican and black man had got in a big fight in the cell a few days before I got there. Bill and I talked and became good friends, I let Bill know I read the Bible three times in my life and he was intrigued. So intrigued that he wanted me to show him how to understand the Bible. So that evening when they let us out our cells I went and got me a bible and that's what I did. I had Bible study with Bill in our cell and gave him the interpretation of the Bible in a way that he could understand. A few days had gone by and all I was concerned with was getting my commissary with my pencil and paper, so I could pick back up with my book and finish it up while I was in jail. While I waited I stayed reading my bible and planning on what I was going to do when I got released. Bill would always ask me why I didn't go out of the cell and watch TV and hit the rec yard. I told Bill in a serious manner that my spirit was too strong and I wanted to lay low. I let Bill know that I didn't know anyone in our unit, but I could guarantee that I knew people that they knew and people would draw to me and it would be too much. Bill laughed with a smile and said that's what's up. That night as I was reading my bible to Bill he was so into it that I normally would read three chapters and stop to interpret it to him, but when I asked did he want me to keep reading, he looked up and said, "Yeah yeah yeah, read some more." The next day, I was in my cell I looked out and saw that there were new inmates in the unit, as there were always new inmates coming and going. But I noticed a new face that looked familiar, a guy I went to junior high school with. When I popped out my cell and got closer, it was him, my good friend named Sam. When Sam saw me his face lit up like a light bulb and he said, "Marc, damn boy it's been years." Sam and I hadn't seen each other in over fifteen years. As we talked it was like the whole unit was watching us, especially me because up to this point I had been silent and low key. Sam was just like me, but totally opposite too, in the fact that he knew a lot of people in the jail and he was always building with other inmates. Once Sam knew I was into music and had my own company, he was down. Sam was plugging me with everybody, rappers and dope plugs from all ethnic backgrounds. It was so bad that dudes start calling me OG in my unit. When I told Sam my company name was Orchestr8ed Hitz, that's all he kept screaming in the jail was Orchestr8ed Hitz. I finally got my canteen and started finishing my book while I was in. On or about my sixth day in I got called to the C/O's desk for my official release date papers and I was in awe. Out of the thirty-day sentence, I was credited two days served when I got locked up and thirteen days taken off. I stopped and prayed to God because this was a miracle of grace. I had been up all night reading my Bible and I could feel the anointment of God on me so strong that I knew I had power in me and I wanted to let his power heal others. As they were calling people to the court that morning I was looking out my cell and a dude in the cell across from me was going to court. So I asked him his name and told him he was going to be going home. Then I grabbed his hand from my cell and prayed for him in the name of Jesus that he would be going home. As we finished praying, he looked at me and said thank you for that bruh. While staring out my cell I saw another inmate that knew my celli Bill, his name was Blue. Blue was cool, he had a grey eye because he had got stabbed in it, so he looked savage, but his heart was good. So I asked Blue was he going to court and he said yeah, so I reached out my hand and prayed for him and I told him he was going home. Blue told me thank you and they all went off for court that morning. Later that evening I was outside in the rec yard and I and an older inmate were talking and he mentioned that he had a bad back pain and I mentioned that when I was in pain how my chiropractor had fixed my pain. We kept talking and I thought nothing of it, when I went back to my cell, the inmates from the court were returning from that morning. I saw the first guy I prayed for and I asked him how it went. He looked at me and he lit up with a smile and said, "Yes, I'm going home." "Thank you, thank you." I let him know I was only listening to God and I'm glad he was going home. After he walked away, I knew the power of God had blessed him and it made me totally complete to know he used me to help someone. I saw Blue about ten minutes later and asked him, "How it go with you in court?" He told me that they gave him a bond and he was going home. I was happy for them both, but happier that my faith stepped out and I was seeing Gods will. I knew I was doing what God wanted me to do and as crazy as it sounds, I knew that this is where he wanted me to be. I went in my cell and laid down to get ready for the count. When they called for all inmates to return back to their cells for count, my celli Bill came in from out the yard and said, "They talking about you out there man." So I said what you mean? Bill said that everyone was saying how I was praying people home and healing people. I smiled, but I didn't celebrate, I knew it was God and I was only doing his work. A few days after that I was transferred out of the processing unit and into general population. For my last week in jail, I stayed networking and I wrote two more chapters of The Tupac Code. I prayed another guy I met home when he went to court and stayed reading my Bible.

After serving my time I was released and came home with an acting career and a distribution deal. I had a new start with life and I was grateful that God gave me another chance.

CHAPTER 18

REVELATION

(Timothy 4:16)

Take heed unto thyself and unto the doctrine; continue in them: For in doing this thou shalt both save thyself and them that hear thee.

The day I came home from jail I knew I was in the hands of God and on his time. I was grateful to his mercy because I was a true witness that he lives. After a year of losing everything I owned and reflecting on my troubles, I came back home to my mother's house to rebuild my life over again and to fulfill Gods purpose in my life. From the time I had started pursuing my vision of being a rap artist until now it had been more than twenty years that passed. In that time of me reaching for success and fortune through rap, I had seen fame and fortune through life. I had seen a lot of lives lost due to the lifestyle of rap and hip hop. I had suffered the pain of living and surviving in the present-day culture. The culture that inspires rap, the lifestyle that my people kill and die in and the aftermath of drug abuse and broken homes. For the first time in my life

I felt God was giving me a small piece of his understanding because when I looked at what I lost and what I didn't have anymore it made me weak, but when I looked at everything in my life God had brought me through and the doors of opportunity he had for me, it gave me strength. From the time I was born, I had a natural and true gift and I was always blessed with talent. But from the first time I saw and heard Tupac Shakur I was inspired to live life, to seek truth and righteousness and justice in my life. Just as John the Baptist made way for Jesus Christ, I believe that Tupac leads the way for Marc Shyst. Just as the doors I walk through will lead the way of righteousness to another leader of our next generation. There is only one God who created one world and he gave his one and only son Jesus to die for our sins. There will only be one Tupac Shakur, Tupac in all his wisdom knew his calling and knew his fate. He also knew he wouldn't save the world, but he knew he would spark the brain that would save the world. This book you have read is an introduction to that brain that was sparked, the man who was called and the spirit in hip hop that was sent. There have been a lot of rappers who have tried to mimic Tupac and even sound like him, but mimicking and copying him is not the code that embodies him. It's spiritual substance, its knowledge of self as an African American, its political awareness, it's a rebellion of police corruption, it's standing up and being a voice for the streets and it's the sufferings of Jesus Christ. I believe we all have a little Tupac in us, it's just that many don't know what it is. God has blessed me to see things many don't and hear the messages of the secrets of heaven. I cracked the code and I call it The Tupac Code. At my lowest point in life, it was clear that I was at my strongest point. As I prepared to finish this book, I just received a call from Edi Amin from Tupac's group The Outlaws. He has agreed to do a feature with me and it has given me hope in the future of prophecy. I have been blessed to star in a few independent films. I have played background work on Creed 2 and recently released a brand new single called Social Media Love on my distribution deal I recently signed. My life has just begun and The Tupac Code lives in me. It's the independence of ownership, its black empowerment through the political office and black economics. It's using our talents to inspire a nation to do right by each other in a time of wickedness. There are a lot of rappers and

musicians in this day and age that have had success
because of the doors Tupac opened. So at the height of my
calling, my greatest empowerment that I could give was to
give the world one of the greatest stories never heard and
give definition to The Tupac Code. I pray my book has
inspired you and I pray my future is a witness to you that
God lives and his prophecy is real. I am just a servant and
my future is in the hands of God. In a world of darkness, I
give it light. May your soul be saved and your prayers are
answered for the goodness of the will of God, and may you
forever live by The Code, The Tupac Code. May every soul
that reads this book be inspired to follow your dreams and
have the power to believe. May the blessings you prayed
to God for come to you, in Jesus name (Amen).

www.ingramcontent.com/pod-product-compliance
Lightning Source LLC
Chambersburg PA
CBHW051849090426
42811CB00034B/2264/J